THE WORLD'S GREATEST

HOTELS
RESORTS
+SPAS

TRAVEL
+LEISURE

THE WORLD'S GREATEST
HOTELS
RESORTS
+SPAS

THIRD EDITION

TRAVEL
+LEISURE
BOOKS

AMERICAN EXPRESS PUBLISHING CORPORATION
NEW YORK

TRAVEL + LEISURE
THE WORLD'S GREATEST HOTELS, RESORTS, AND SPAS
THIRD EDITION

Editors Laura Begley, Nina Willdorf
Project Editor Mario López-Cordero
Assistant Managing Editor Meeghan Truelove
Art Director Sandra Garcia
Photo Editor Robyn Lange
Reporters Hillary Geronemus, Darrell Hartman,
Dulcy Israel, Carolina Miranda, Maria Shollenbarger,
Bunny Wong
Copy Editors Stephen Clair, Mike Iveson,
Margaret Nussey, Shazdeh Omari,
Kathy Roberson, Dara Stewart, Ellie Sweeney
Production Editor David Richey
Researchers Robert Alford, Adam Bisno,
Anila Churi, Kristina Ensminger, Angela Fleury,
Catesby Holmes, Kathryn O'Shea-Evans,
Mary Staub
Assistant Book Editors Tanvi Chheda, Alison Goran
Proofreader Susan Groarke

TRAVEL + LEISURE
Editor-in-Chief Nancy Novogrod
Creative Director Nora Sheehan
Executive Editor Jennifer Barr
Managing Editor Michael S. Cain
Arts/Research Editor Mario R. Mercado
Copy Chief Lee Magill
Photo Editor Katie Dunn
Production Director Rosalie Abatemarco Samat
Production Manager Ayad Sinawi

AMERICAN EXRESS PUBLISHING
CORPORATION
President, C.E.O. Ed Kelly
S.V.P., Chief Marketing Officer Mark V. Stanich
**C.F.O., S.V.P., Corporate Development &
Operations** Paul B. Francis
V.P., Books & Products Marshall Corey
Senior Marketing Manager Bruce Spanier
Assistant Marketing Manager Sarah Ross
Director of Fulfillment Phil Black
**Manager of Customer Experience &
Product Development** Charles Graver
Business Manager Tom Noonan
Corporate Production Manager Stuart Handelman

Cover design by Sandra Garcia
Cover photograph by Chris Wise
Overleaf: A pool at the Chedi Muscat, in Oman.
Opposite: The façade of the Petit Hotel d'Hafa,
in Sayulita, Mexico.
Page 11: A guest room at the Oasis, in
San Miguel de Allende, Mexico.

ISBN-10 1-932624-28-7
ISBN-13 978-1-932624-28-1
ISSN 1559-0372

Published by
American Express Publishing Corporation
1120 Avenue of the Americas
New York, New York 10036

Distributed by DK Publishing, Inc.
375 Hudson Street, New York, New York 10014

Manufactured in the United States of America

CONTENTS

CONTENTS

CONTENTS

INTRODUCTION

I CONFESS I'M A HOTEL DEPENDENT, AND I CAN MOVE from elation to despair in the course of one 24-hour stay. A wake-up call that never arrives, a breakfast tray delivered as I'm rushing out the door, a wet towel that lingers by the shower throughout the day—these can overcome the pleasures of even the most attractive accommodations. But when it works—when the stars are aligned and service, setting, and housekeeping are all in top form—there's nothing better or more deeply relaxing than throwing my short-term fate into the hands of a team of experts. There's bliss in a good hotel.

And one thing my years as the editor-in-chief of *Travel + Leisure* have taught me is that legions of people feel exactly the same way I do—and if you are holding this hotel- and resort-obsessed volume in your hands, you are most likely among them. Each month in the pages of *Travel + Leisure* we present the latest and best information about the properties that distinguish themselves from the pack—whether recent arrivals or enduring favorites. Our editors, writers, and international network of correspondents are always on the prowl for the best places, sending out all-points bulletins when they uncover a pressworthy expression of excellence in the hospitality world, which then becomes a story.

The process of assembling this book is quite simple: T+L editors comb through a year's worth of issues in order to come up with our favorite properties—the most newsworthy, most directional, most appealing. The goal is to capture the opportunities and excitement of travel by highlighting the hotel experience, and to make choosing a destination an easy and interesting adventure in itself. For instance, in our third annual compendium of *The World's Greatest Hotels, Resorts, and Spas*, we preview the options for those planning a no-expenses-spared trip to Tokyo by profiling the crop of new name-brand luxury hotels. If southern France is the destination and low-key your style, we offer a constellation of modern but no less charming French country inns. There are New Zealand lodges, Asian island retreats, intimate hotels in Rome with spectacular views, and even a new generation of supercool motels in the U.S.

As always, we are proud to present the results of *Travel + Leisure*'s World's Best Awards survey, which you'll find in Part II. Each year our readers speak to us in a voice that's loud and clear about their favorite hotel choices, which always tells us more than that alone. The latest results reveal a passion for India, with three properties scoring in the top 15, including the No. 1 hotel overall—Udaipur's Oberoi Udaivilas. To make the book more useful still, we've added a Resources section, beginning on page 216, that enables you to find the type of hotel you're looking for (beach resort, mountain lodge, romantic retreat), and easily research all the book's properties by location.

Appropriately enough, I am sitting at a desk in a spectacular Paris hotel as I write this intro-duction. (Far be it from me to tell you which one.) In spite of my happiness right now, my search continues for the hotel that is the fairest of them all. Of course, I have no intention of finding it—I'm having too much fun looking.

NANCY NOVOGROD

562

UNITED STATES+CANADA

The restored 1957
façade of the Orbit In,
in Palm Springs.

Castle Hill's lawn,
on a promontory
overlooking the
Atlantic Ocean and
Narragansett Bay.
Right: A beach
cottage at the resort.

CASTLE HILL INN & RESORT

Newport, Rhode Island

IN 1874, MINING MAGNATE ALEXANDER AGASSIZ, GENTLEMAN explorer and part-time oceanographer, had a sprawling summer house built just outside of Newport. It was an ideal setting for a man who'd made strides in the field of marine biology. Set on a small peninsula where the Atlantic meets Narragansett Bay, it was, and still is, a perfect spot from which to observe marine mammals. Long since put into service as a resort, Agassiz's Victorian mansion has never lost its aristocratic charm. It has nine guest rooms and suites, the most dramatic occupying a mahogany-trimmed turret with a 360-degree view and a soaking tub overlooking the sea. Ten understated wood-shingle cottages—whitewashed wainscoting, apron-front sinks, beach glass–colored fabrics—offer a more low-key alternative just steps from the sand.

590 Ocean Dr., Newport, R.I.; 888/466-1355 or 401/849-3800; castlehillinn.com; doubles from $$

Right: Winvian's Seth Bird House, which has dining rooms and a suite. Below: The Beaver Lodge's foyer. Opposite: A bed at the Beaver Lodge, flanked by tree-trunk support beams, with a beaver lodge overhead.

WINVIAN

Morris, Connecticut

ON A SPRAWLING COLONIAL ESTATE IN NORTH-western Connecticut, an over-the-top new resort called Winvian has opened its doors. The conceptual project reflects the combined efforts of owner Maggie Smith and her daughter Heather, who, with the assistance of David Sellers, a former professor at the Yale School of Architecture, asked 15 architects and designers to unleash their fertile imaginations and create a collection of 18 idiosyncratic cottages. One structure is made of boulders; another is a tree house set 35 feet off the ground. There is a suite built around an old Coast Guard helicopter, while a cottage called the Beaver Lodge has an actual beaver lodge suspended from the ceiling. Comfort, however, is never sacrificed in the name of design. Rooms come with fluffy robes, steam showers, and fully stocked bars.

155 Alain White Rd., Morris, Conn.; 800/735-2478 or 860/567-9600; winvian.com; doubles from $$$$$, including meals

INN AT KENT FALLS

Kent, Connecticut

The living room of the Inn at Kent Falls, built in 1741.

STAYING AT THE SIX-ROOM INN AT KENT FALLS is like visiting your stylish country friends who are partial to plush towels and slipcovered furniture. The inn strikes a balance between Colonial-era restraint and modern-day comfort—the floors in the renovated 18th-century farmhouse still creak atmospherically, but rooms include free Wi-Fi. In the mornings, owner Ira Goldspiel, a former fashion executive, and manager Glen Sherman serve breakfasts of homemade granola and brioche French toast. The room to book is the Lakes Suite, which has a claw-foot bathtub and a fireplace lit with candles instead of logs.

107 Kent Cornwall Rd.; Kent, Conn.; 860/927-3197; theinnatkentfalls.com; doubles from $, including breakfast.

6 COLUMBUS

New York, New York

WITH A FAUX FUR–CLAD LOBBY, *JETSONS*-STYLE LEATHER CHAIRS, and mod prints by photographer Guy Bourdin, 6 Columbus presents an opportunity to revel in 1960's nostalgia. The hotel's 88 rooms—designed by Steven Sclaroff, the man behind the look of the Kate Spade stores—have Eames bedside lamps, groovy backlit circular mirrors in navy-tiled bathrooms, custom linen–dressed beds, and lots of teak paneling. An outpost of downtown's perennially packed Blue Ribbon Sushi Bar & Grill, off the lobby, is a popular spot where you may find yourself sipping saketinis beside media moguls from the neighboring Time Warner Center.

6 Columbus Circle, New York, N.Y.; 877/626-5862 or 212/204-3000; thompsonhotels.com; doubles from $$.

The 6 Columbus reception area.

BOWERY HOTEL

New York, New York

HOTELIERS SEAN MacPHERSON AND ERIC GOODE—the team behind
New York's Maritime Hotel—are breathing new life into Manhattan's once-desolate Bowery with their 135-room Bowery Hotel.
Entering the lobby is like stepping into a pre-Raphaelite painting:
a Gothic fireplace, Oriental rugs over a Moroccan-tiled floor.
Rooms are pure vintage-repro, down to the beadboard ceilings;
toiletries from the storied Bigelow & Co. Apothecary line marble
washstands. Those expecting a dose of New York attitude will
be disappointed by the friendly staff. There's plenty of native
flavor, however, at the Italian restaurant, Gemma, where focaccia-
bread pizzas are drizzled with truffle oil, and the bar is reliably
thronged by those city denizens known as Beautiful People.

335 Bowery, New York, N.Y.;
212/505-9100; theboweryhotel.com;
doubles from $$$

Bowery Hotel owners
Sean MacPherson and
Eric Goode in the lobby.

Shinn Estate's Vineyard West room, with a cedar-paneled ceiling.

SHINN ESTATE FARMHOUSE

Mattituck, New York

2000 Oregon Rd., Mattituck, N.Y.; 631/804-0367; shinnfarmhouse.com; doubles from $, including breakfast

THE NORTH FORK OF LONG ISLAND—A 30-MILE STRIP of oceanside plains dotted with farms and boutique wineries—is the quiet alternative to the nearby Hamptons. Overlooking trellises of grapevines, the four-room Shinn Estate Farmhouse is a place of respite for urban epicures. Proprietors David Page and Barbara Shinn gave the circa-1880 building a makeover last year, and their sunny B&B—with floors lined in pine, fir, and oak—exudes a city-meets-country grace. The breakfasts showcase seasonal produce, and maple bacon that Page cures himself. But the main event here is the wine, from a crisp rosé to a fruity Sauvignon Blanc–Sémillon blend, all produced in small batches on the estate.

Kate Pierson
in the kitchen
of a suite at
Lazy Meadow.

KATE'S LAZY MEADOW MOTEL

Mount Tremper, New York

AT KATE'S LAZY MEADOW MOTEL, THE QUIRKY personality of Kate Pierson, one of the lead singers for the B-52's, shines through in every detail. The nine suites will transport you to a time when Formica, Tupperware, and the Avon Lady were young, and lime green and burnt orange were viable decorative options. In the back, five vintage aluminum Airstream trailers are stocked with barbecues and tiki torches. Pierson employs only a small staff, so you're somewhat on your own; there is no daily maid service, for example. However, all of the groovy accoutrements result in an authentically personal, utterly unique place to stay.

5191 Rte. 28, Mount Tremper, N.Y.;
845/688-7200; lazymeadow.com; doubles from $

A sitting room in a Hotel Fauchère suite.

HOTEL FAUCHÈRE

Milford, Pennsylvania

LOCATED IN THE TOWN OF MILFORD, PENNSYLVANIA, 75 miles west of New York City, the Hotel Fauchère has long been a getaway for boldface names. Charlie Chaplin, Andrew Carnegie, and Babe Ruth have all laid their heads at the 1880 inn, originally opened by Louis Fauchère, once a master chef at the famed Delmonico's in Manhattan. Though the hotel pays homage to its long history (note the vintage European menus in the restaurant), it is very much a 21st-century hideaway. Owners recently completed a five-year renovation that preserved original decorative touches such as chestnut floors and a walnut-and-mahogany banister. By contrast, the 16 guest rooms are contemporary retreats, with rain showers, radiant-heat floors, and Frette linens.

401 Broad St., Milford, Pa.; 570/409-1212; hotelfauchere.com; doubles from $ $

INN AT 202 DOVER

Easton, Maryland

The Inn at 202 Dover, near the Chesapeake Bay.

IN 2005, RONALD AND SHELBY MITCHELL—a former D.C. ad exec and lawyer—discovered a deteriorating 1874 Colonial-style mansion, which they restored to the tune of $2 million. Open since 2006, the Inn at 202 Dover's four suites are now tastefully decorated with velvet-covered settees, toile curtains and pelmets, and antiques such as a bamboo canopy bed. The genteel touches are accompanied by modern amenities; all rooms are equipped with flat-screen TV's, steam showers, and jet-stream tubs. Each morning, Ronald prepares breakfast (orange croissant French toast with ham, or vegetable quiche), which he serves on Wedgwood china in the glass-ceilinged conservatory; and each evening, his homemade chocolate chip cookies await guests in their rooms.

202 E. Dover St., Easton, Md.; 866/450-7600; innat202dover.com; doubles from $$

Keswick Hall, as seen from its Arnold Palmer–designed golf course.

KESWICK HALL

Keswick, Virginia

THE FOOTHILLS OF VIRGINIA'S BLUE RIDGE MOUNTAINS, south and west of Washington, D.C., are a playground for the city's old guard, their horses, and their beagles. With its laird-of-the-manor grandeur, no place evokes the regional esprit like Keswick Hall. In a stately Tuscan-style structure originally built in 1912, its 48 guest rooms are decorated with a mix of hunt-club prints, canopy beds, polished armoires, and Chippendale chairs. There are hints of fun: one room holds a framed collection of Best in Show ribbons that somebody's poodle won. Fossett's, the swag-festooned restaurant, serves some of Virginia's most compelling food—quail with chanterelles, rockfish with mussels and fava beans—with bottles from up-and-coming local wineries: King Family Vineyards, Blenheim Vineyards, and Kluge Estate.

701 Club Dr., Keswick, Va.; 800/274-5391 or 434/979-3440; keswick.com; doubles from $$

CASA MORADA

Islamorada, Florida

CASA MORADA, IN THE FLORIDA KEYS, IS THE brainchild of partners Lauren Abrams, Terry Ford, and Heide Praver Werthamer, who collectively spent 24 years picking up the tricks of the trade while working at various Ian Schrager hotels. Ninety minutes south of Miami, the tranquil, 1.7-acre property seems a thousand miles from the hustle of Ocean Drive. Casa Morada's 16 suites are large and luminous, bright-white and breezy, punctuated with area rugs and orchids in clay pots. Mexican antiques are juxtaposed with modern custom-designed tables and beds. Each suite has a private outdoor space with chaises or Adirondack-style chairs. Jutting out from the small island into Florida Bay is a spacious pavilion on stilts, the perfect perch from which to watch for manatees and enjoy a late-afternoon glass of wine.

136 Madeira Rd., Islamorada, Fla.;
888/881-3030 or 305/664-0044; casamorada.com;
doubles from $$

Casa Morada's
overwater pavilion.

An original bank vault behind the Hotel Icon's front desk.

REGISTRATION

HOTEL ICON

Houston, Texas

IT'D BE TOUGH TO FIND A MORE IDEAL SITE for an intimately scaled grand hotel than the nearly century-old landmark Union National Bank in downtown Houston. The 126 rooms and nine penthouse suites marry luxurious touches (marble-countered bathrooms, high ceilings, rain showers) with business-friendly accoutrements (work spaces with ergonomic chairs, laptop-accommodating safes). Next to a light rail stop in the historic center, the hotel offers easy access to the Houston Grand Opera and the theater district. Though everything is a short stroll away, a complimentary car service awaits those not inclined to walk.

220 Main St., Houston, Tex.; 800/970-4266 or 713/224-4266; hotelicon.com; doubles from $.

Blinded by the Light
(1991), a photograph by
Yasumasa Morimura,
in a sitting area in
the Chambers lobby.

CHAMBERS HOTEL

Minneapolis, Minnesota

ON THE HEELS OF MINNEAPOLIS'S REMARKABLE
architectural double shot—Herzog & de Meuron's
Walker Art Center expansion and Jean Nouvel's
Guthrie Theater—the David Rockwell–designed
Chambers packs enough theatricality to rival both.
Inside, a desiccated bull's head by Damien Hirst
looms behind the front desk, a ground-floor gallery
showcases a provocative roster of artists such as
Angela Strassheim and Jude Tallichet, and in-room
plasma televisions play a three-hour loop of video
art. In the evenings, crowds of glammed-up theater-
goers, twentysomethings in T-shirts, and after-work
professionals gather at the rooftop bar or Chambers
Kitchen, run by Jean-Georges Vongerichten. The 60
rooms are minimalist but comfortable, with black-
leather headboards, feather beds topped with buttery-
white sheets, and the requisite copy of *Wallpaper*.
But it's the staff, with their refreshing lack of design-
hotel attitude, that ultimately wins over guests.

901 Hennepin Ave., Minneapolis, Minn.; 877/767-6990 or
612/767-6900; chambersminneapolis.com; doubles from $$

RED MOUNTAIN SPA

St. George, Utah

1275 E. Red Mountain Circle, St. George, Utah; 800/407-3002 or 435/673-4905; redmountainspa.com; doubles from $$$

RINGED BY A TRIO OF NATURAL ATTRACTIONS—Snow, Zion, and Bryce canyons—the Red Mountain Spa devotes as much attention to fitness as to pampering. A sample day can include hiking, biking, and rock climbing, as well as locally inspired spa treatments; the Canyon Sage Warm Stone Massage, for instance, uses energy-rich indigenous rocks. Rounding out the wellness experience is the restaurant, which serves regionally inflected, healthful dishes such as prickly-pear barbecue-glazed pork tenderloin. The 82 rooms and villas were renovated in 2006 with an updated Southwestern design that blends in seamlessly with the red rocks and lava fields right outside the door.

The villas at Red Mountain Spa, framed by the peaks after which it's named.

Inside the spa at the Four Seasons Hotel Westlake Village.

FOUR SEASONS HOTEL WESTLAKE VILLAGE

Westlake Village, California

BY PAIRING A LUXURY HOTEL WITH A STATE-OF-THE-art medical facility, this collaboration between Four Seasons and the California Health & Longevity Institute—located in a San Fernando Valley suburb only 17 miles from Malibu—introduces a new level of service (and seriousness) to the spa experience. While guest rooms are dressed in Pierre Deux fabrics, the spa takes a hard-science approach to health. A three-day package includes a physical that incorporates cancer and choles-terol screenings, a cardiac risk analysis, and a test that examines your DNA's damage and repair mechanisms. More-traditional treatments— Swedish and shiatsu massage—are also on the menu for those simply looking to relax.

2 Dole Dr., Westlake Village, Calif.; 800/332-3442 or 818/575-3000; fourseasons.com; doubles from $$

CULVER HOTEL

Culver City, California

LOS ANGELES–AREA PAINTERS AND CURATORS HAVE transformed the industrial spaces of Culver City into a thriving art colony, and the metamorphosis at the Culver Hotel mirrors that resurgence. When the six-story property first opened in 1924, it quickly became a favored haunt of creative types. (Virtually the whole cast of Munchkins moved in during the filming of *The Wizard of Oz*.) After a decline that coincided with the fall of the city's film studios, the place was renovated in the late 1990's. The lobby was restored to its old-Hollywood glam: marble floors, mahogany-paneled walls, and a potted palm–dotted piano bar. The 46 antique-filled rooms are up next—their dated pastel color schemes are getting freshened up with walls and fabrics in a cool gray palette.

9400 Culver Blvd., Culver City, Calif.; 310/838-7963; culverhotel.com; doubles from $

The entrance of the Renaissance-Revival Culver Hotel.

The saltwater pool at the Orbit In.

ORBIT IN

Palm Springs, California

*562 W. Arenas Rd., Palm Springs, Calif.;
877/996-7248 or 760/323-3585; orbitin.com;
doubles from $$, including breakfast*

A MODERNIST 1957 STRUCTURE, THE ORBIT IN HAD BEEN the object of benign neglect for decades when it was purchased by its former owners, who restored the Space Race–era exteriors and filled it with period-perfect furniture by masters such as Harry Bertoia and Eero Saarinen. Current proprietors Kevin and Jinni Miller recently updated the property with flat-screen TV's and Bose radios. All nine studio-style rooms open onto private patios; four are equipped with white enameled kitchenettes. In a garden off the motel's entrance, a large whirlpool with an adjacent fire pit provides warmth on cool desert nights, and guests enjoy retro cocktails while Frank Sinatra croons in the background.

A Calistoga Ranch
guest lodge. Opposite:
The hotel's lobby.

CALISTOGA RANCH

Calistoga, California

SURROUNDED BY NAPA VALLEY VINEYARDS AND OAKS, Calistoga Ranch, run by the company behind nearby Auberge du Soleil, is like a summer camp for pampered adults, with copper-trimmed cedar cabins serving as stylish bunkhouses. No cars are allowed on the 157-acre property, so guests—including robed couples en route to the Bathhouse spa— are escorted about in golf carts. Morning yoga takes place in the wine cave, and after a soak in a mineral pool, guests keep warm under handwoven chenille throws in front of outdoor fireplaces. Staff will pour you an in-room tubful of the restorative mud that has been drawing wellness seekers to the area for 150 years. If you are feeling squeamish, try the 90-minute Cabernet Classic, a grapeseed scrub and grapeseed-oil massage that makes creative use of the Valley's most famous crop.

580 Lommel Rd., Calistoga, Calif.; 800/942-4220 or 707/254-2800; calistogaranch.com; doubles from $$$

The Drake's exterior. Left: The bar in the main lounge.

DRAKE HOTEL

Toronto, Canada

TORONTO'S WEST QUEEN WEST is a neighborhood in flux, where appliance stores, art galleries, and places like Camera, a screening-room bar owned by filmmaker Atom Egoyan, exist cheek by jowl. In 2001, when Canadian entrepreneur Jeff Stober first walked into the Drake Hotel, a former flophouse on a gritty stretch, he saw its potential and set about fashioning a hub for the area's creative types. The style of the 19 rooms is beyond eclectic: floral wallpaper, sock dolls crafted by a local artist, transparent ottomans with visible springs, ladders leading up to an overhead storage space. Downstairs, the dining-room walls are covered in trippy flocked Rorschach blots, and the lounge has leather booths and red velvet banquettes. The hotel employs an in-house curator who arranges shows in the lobby exhibition space and manages an artist-in-residence program. Permanent art displays are peppered throughout the building, from a light installation made from bicycle parts in the café to a *Bums and Chests* piece made from postcards in a men's lavatory.

1150 Queen St. W., Toronto, Ontario, Canada; 866/372-5386 or 416/531-5042; thedrakehotel.ca; doubles from $

HÔTEL LE ST.-JAMES

Montreal, Canada

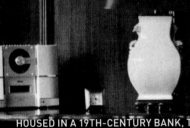

HOUSED IN A 19TH-CENTURY BANK, THE HÔTEL
Le St.-James is a Gilded Age fantasy in the
heart of bustling Vieux-Montréal. Each of its
60 rooms is artfully crammed with treasures:
oriental carpets, Italian oil paintings, Ming
vases, and outsize four-poster beds. Modern
comforts (plasma televisions, Molton Brown
toiletries) offset all the grandeur. Guests
can have traditional afternoon tea care
of Mariage Frères in the Grand Salon, a lofty
room with two stately staircases and a
mezzanine converted from a bankers' hall.
Downstairs, the spa takes similar advantage
of the hotel's past life: you can book a
massage in a former vault with sky-high
ceilings and onyx floors.

355 Rue St. Jacques, Montreal, Quebec, Canada;
866/841-3111 or 514/841-3111; hotellestjames.com;
doubles from $$

A canopy bed
in the Hôtel
Le St.-James.

Room No. 326, with wide-plank wood floors, at Auberge St.-Antoine. Left: The entrance to the hotel's restaurant, Panache.

AUBERGE ST.-ANTOINE

Quebec City, Canada

world's best

THE STATELY 19TH-CENTURY FAÇADE of the St.-Antoine doesn't give away what's behind it: a modern boutique hotel, complete with sharply dressed concierges and an up-tempo lobby soundtrack. But the history of the former maritime warehouse is inscribed in its walls. Shards of blue delft and ancient vial stoppers—all uncovered during the renovation—are displayed in vitrines throughout the lobby. In brisk weather, blazes roar in the lounge's sleek stone fireplaces. In front of them, children play backgammon while their art director parents relax on pillow-strewn sofas, drinking wine. Past-present juxtapositions continue in the rooms and suites, furnished with a mix of European antiques and contemporary pieces; the bathrooms have huge soaking tubs. The rustic-chic restaurant, Panache, in a barnlike room with hand-hewn beams, stands out for its simple Québécois interpretations of seasonal foods: tender venison rib or hare with yellow beets cooked *en cocotte*.

8 Rue St.-Antoine, Quebec City, Quebec, Canada; 888/692-2211 or 418/692-2211; saint-antoine.com; doubles from $

MANOIR HOVEY

North Hatley, Canada

The façade of Manoir Hovey.

THE LAKESIDE VILLAGE OF NORTH HATLEY—87 miles east of Montreal and 20 miles north of the U.S. border—is the summer destination of the province's heavy hitters (the premier of Quebec) and epicures, who come for locally produced raw-milk cheeses, foie gras, and apple cider pressed by Benedictine monks. Tempting these discriminating palates is Manoir Hovey, an 1899 Georgian inn and restaurant on Lake Massawippi. Chef Roland Ménard runs its kitchen, and for the past 27 years he's been preparing such gratifying dishes as seared duck breast with pan-roasted wild mushrooms. Upstairs, the hotel's 39 rooms are equally comforting, with bold checkered fabrics, canopy beds, and, in some instances, fireplaces.

575 Hovey Rd., North Hatley, Quebec, Canada; 800/661-2421 or 819/842-2421; manoirhovey.com; doubles from $$, including breakfast and dinner

A daybed overlooking
the Caribbean
Sea at Casa Magna,
in Tulum, Mexico.

MEXICO+ CENTRAL+ SOUTH AMERICA

HACIENDA SAN ANGEL

Puerto Vallarta, Mexico

A colonial-style suite at the Hacienda San Angel.

IN THE 1960'S, PUERTO VALLARTA CAPTIVATED THE LIKES OF John Huston and Elizabeth Taylor, and today the city center, where vendors negotiate sidewalks while balancing trays of empanadas on their heads, is recapturing that allure. Amid the bustle is the Hacienda San Angel, which is only a couple of blocks from the busy waterfront *malecón,* but feels miles away. The colonial-style hotel has been fashioned from five houses linked by gardens, walkways, and bougainvillea-draped courtyards. In the 16 suites, 17th-century wooden saints hold court against a background of colorful Mexican tiles and antique European crosses. Many rooms also have terraces where you can glimpse the wrought-iron crown of Our Lady of Guadalupe Cathedral and the Bay of Banderas beyond.

336 Miramar, Col. Centro, Puerto Vallarta, Mexico; 877/815-6594 or 52-322/222-2692; haciendasanangel.com; doubles from $$, including breakfast

A sitting area in Verana's Studio bungalow, above the Bay of Banderas.

VERANA

Yelapa, Mexico

Yelapa, Jalisco, Mexico; 800/530-7176 or 310/360-0155; verana.com; doubles from $$

YELAPA LIES SOUTH OF PUERTO VALLARTA, and is accessible only by boat, by mountain bike, or on foot. To reach the Verana hotel from the shore, you take a 15-minute donkey ride through steep jungle—a little jostly, as you'd expect, but also very exciting. The landscape opens to reveal the bay below and, past the hotel, the Sierra Madre Occidental mountains. Like the views, the eight guest rooms are both exhilarating and peaceful. Heinz Legler, the hotel's owner and architect, loves half-walls, but he loves no walls even more. His wife, Veronique Lievre, decorated the interiors with wicker chairs, George Nelson lighting, twig furniture made on-site, and found objects like tide-smoothed pebbles. Their restaurant is one of the best in the area, serving such dishes as red snapper grilled whole and lemongrass crème brûlée.

PETIT HOTEL D'HAFA

Sayulita, Mexico

THE SIX-ROOM PETIT HOTEL D'HAFA is a winsome bit of Morocco in the middle of Sayulita, a fishing village that's also known for some of Mexico's best surfing waves. Owners Christophe Mignot and his Spanish wife, Marina (unofficially the best-looking couple in town), have built a hotel with character: barrel-vaulted ceilings, chartreuse polished-cement floors, and pierced-tin wall lights in the shape of angel wings. Straw mats are stenciled with hearts, crescents, and stylized flowers; bathroom sinks have hand-tempered copper basins. Even the walkways exhibit charm—bright red hearts against the blue painted floorboards call to mind stepping-stones.

55 Calle Revolución, Sayulita, Nayarit, Mexico; 52-329/291-3806; sayulitalife.com; doubles from $

A Pop art–inspired walkway leads to a suite in the Petit Hotel d'Hafa.

One of several pools at the Four Seasons Resort Punta Mita.

FOUR SEASONS RESORT PUNTA MITA

Punta Mita, Mexico

*Punta Mita, Bahía de Banderas, Mexico;
800/332-3442 or 52-329/291-6000;
fourseasons.com; doubles from $$$*

world's best

DOMINATING A LUSH PENINSULA ON THE Bahía de Banderas, the 173-room Four Seasons Resort Punta Mita is just one part of an extravagant 1,500-acre planned development. Here, members of the emerging "entourage travel" market can book a 9,150-square-foot private casita with five bedrooms, a media room, fitness center, and a "personal host" who seemingly never sleeps. But standard rooms and suites are nothing to shake a stick at, with their oversize powder rooms, posh sitting areas, and enormous bathtubs. The resort's curtained poolside cabanas come complete with 42-inch plasma TV's. Pick up the phone and the spa will send someone with all the fixings for a chilled-margarita manicure. At regular intervals, a sunglass doctor pays a visit to clean, tighten, and make scratches disappear from your shades.

THE OASIS

San Miguel de Allende, Mexico

The living room on the first floor of the Oasis.

SEVERAL YEARS AGO IN THE COLONIAL TOWN OF SAN MIGUEL DE ALLENDE, expat Nancy Lane Hooper stumbled upon a collapsed 17th-century mansion with original *cantera*-stone lintels and two-foot-thick walls. She envisioned a tiny East-meets-West retreat, and has turned the ruin into a refuge. Gleaming circular mirrors in chrome frames hang from leather straps, and ogee arches and ornately patterned pillows call to mind a Turkish harem. The four suites have huge beds with 1,000-thread-count sheets, towels as thick as Berber carpets, and sweet little details, such as terra-cotta exfoliants in the bathrooms. The biggest draw is the rooftop terrace, which overlooks the city's pastel domes and filigreed spires; it's a perfect setting for a breakfast of traditional *chilaquiles* (salsa-drenched tortillas and cheese), whipped up by Nellie, the inn's affable cook.

14 Chiquitos, San Miguel de Allende, Mexico; 210/745-1457 or 52-415/154-9250; oasissanmiguel.com; doubles from $$

LA PURIFICADORA

Puebla, Mexico

THE LATEST MASTERPIECE FROM ICONIC MEXICAN architect Ricardo Legorreta: La Purificadora, a thrilling 26-room shot of big-city flair in small-town Puebla. The hotel's name refers to the water-purification plant that once stood on the site; the original 1884 signage is preserved above the entryway. The dramatic three-story, open-air lobby soars over the surrounding colonial-era buildings. Inside, bold purple furnishings stand out in striking contrast against whitewashed walls and gunmetal-gray custom floor tiles. The black-and-white–tiled guest rooms feature glass closets in which clothing seems to float, and glass balconies on which vista-gazing guests seem to levitate. In the ground-floor restaurant, acclaimed Mexico City chef Enrique Olvera creates slicked-up versions of regional standbys like mole-rubbed beef and Mexico's famous pork dish, *cochinita pibil*.

802 Callejón de la 10 Norte, Puebla, Mexico; 52-222/309-1920; lapurificadora.com; doubles from $

A wide staircase leads to the lobby of La Purificadora.

FAIRMONT MAYAKOBA

Playa del Carmen, Mexico

Fairmont Mayakoba's beachfront Las Brisas restaurant.

AS THE RIVIERA MAYA'S FIRST ENVIRONMENTALLY CONSCIOUS golf-and-spa complex, the Fairmont Mayakoba is an eco-friendly alternative to the monolithic resorts clustered along the Caribbean coast of the Yucatán Peninsula. One of four hotels in the huge Mayakoba development that's just a 50-minute drive south of Cancún, the Fairmont sits on 50 acres full of preserved swamps, freshwater lagoons, and canals, and that include a 700-foot-long white-sand beach. There are all the standard resort amenities: five swimming pools, four restaurants—and an aesthetic that pairs thatched roofs and green-and-red fabrics with slatted wooden doors and cool marble floors. The Fairmont combines them with biologically sensitive initiatives such as a Greg Norman–designed golf course certified by Audubon International, and wooden

CASA MAGNA

Tulum, Mexico

A COMPOUND OF THREE-STORY BEACH
houses, Casa Magna was reputedly built
by drug kingpin Pablo Escobar, and
the outlaw couldn't have chosen a more
desirable location than the tiny Yucatán
town of Tulum. The place has been
reincarnated as a small resort hotel,
created by Melissa Perlman, who also
owns the nearby Amansala spa. The
22-room property rises between a dense
jungle and an unspoiled patch of sand
in the Mexican Caribbean. In the larger
house, nine master suites each have
a private terrace, massive poured-
concrete tubs, and ocean views. A room
that once had a dance floor is now filled
with soft sectional couches and Chinese
lanterns. The "Oms" of morning yoga
classes echo in Escobar's former living
room, while at a tiled counter down
the hall, a blender whirs mango, ginger,
and wheatgrass into health shakes.

*Km 9.5, Carr. Tulum-Boca Paila, Tulum, Mexico;
52-998/185-7430; casamagnatulum.com;
doubles from $$ per person, including meals and some
activities*

The reception
area at Casa
Magna. Above:
One of the
property's
guest rooms.

MATACHICA BEACH RESORT

Ambergris Cay, Belize

LAID-BACK AMBERGRIS CAY is just a 20-minute flight from gritty Belize City, but a world apart. The beaches are powdery white, shopping barefoot is encouraged, and the pace is languorous, thanks to the island's car-free roads (locals walk, use electric golf carts, or ride bikes). The newly renovated Matachica Beach Resort, on the private northern side of the island, makes an ideal base: it's sufficiently secluded, but only a short water-taxi ride from lively downtown San Pedro. Not that you'll feel like leaving—the resort has film screenings in its martini lounge and banana-and-brown-sugar facials at the spa. The 14 bungalows are painted in bright Gauguin hues, such as mango and watermelon pink. All offer sea views, air-conditioning, and glass-walled showers surrounded by bamboo plants. The best deals are the four Sea Breeze bungalows—they're a 30-second walk from the water's edge, but cost $120 less than the beachfront casitas.

Ambergris Cay, Belize; 011-501/220-5010; matachica.com; doubles from $$

Matachica's thatch-
roofed lobby.
Opposite: The hotel's
dock looks out
on the Caribbean.

Caracol, a golf clubhouse and restaurant at Four Seasons Peninsula Papagayo. Left: The veranda of a Canopy suite.

FOUR SEASONS RESORT COSTA RICA AT PENINSULA PAPAGAYO

Guanacaste, Costa Rica

Peninsula Papagayo, Guanacaste, Costa Rica; 800/332-3442 or 011-506/696-0000; fourseasons.com; doubles from $$$

world's best **COSTA RICAN ARCHITECT RONALD ZÜRCHER** drew inspiration from butterfly wings and the backs of armadillos in designing the Four Seasons Resort Costa Rica at Peninsula Papagayo, set on a steep hillside between two Pacific beaches. Its 145 rooms and suites are outfitted with indigenous hardwood and stone, sliding louvered doors, verandas, and a palette of deep reds, browns, and yellows; most have plunge pools. Before the resort opened in 2004, getting to this pristine but remote promontory in the northwest of Guanacaste required chartering a plane or navigating bone-rattling potholed roads. Now, major airlines fly direct from the United States to the airport, and newly paved byways make the 29-mile trip from there to the hotel considerably smoother. Conscious of the area's physical splendor, the resort does what it can to minimize its impact. Arnold Palmer created a golf course lauded by Audubon International for its eco-sensitive design; black and gray water is recycled; and during construction, the habitats of local species were left intact.

Tortuga Lodge's main reception area, with a poured–concrete sofa. Right: A guest lounges in front of a Harmony Hotel *palapa*.

TORTUGA LODGE

Tortuguero, Costa Rica

THE FIRST ECO-LODGE TO OPEN NEAR TORTUGUERO National Park, the 22-year-old Tortuga Lodge sits in Costa Rica's "mini-Amazon" on the Atlantic coast, accessible only by boat or plane. The 27 open-air rooms are spread between six modest two-story bungalows that emerge gently from the tropical foliage. Owner Michael Kaye, one of the country's ecotourism pioneers, is always focused on minimizing the lodge's intrusion; he also helped launch a program to protect the local beach, the most important nesting ground in the Western Hemisphere of the endangered Atlantic green sea turtle.

Tortuguero, Costa Rica; 011-506/257-0766; costaricaexpeditions.com; doubles from $

HARMONY HOTEL

Nosara, Costa Rica

THE HARMONY SITS A STONE'S THROW FROM PLAYA Guiones in the sleepy Pacific coast surf town of Nosara. Its 24 rooms are stylishly spare, with vaulted wood ceilings and flowing white fabrics. The environmentally sound property includes a yoga studio and juice bar, recycling bins in each room, and a pool kept clean with salt instead of chlorine. After a day of surfing, guests can relax at the hotel's Healing Centre of Radiant Awakening spa with treatments such as the Banana Bliss moisturizing body mask and the Papaya Delight exfoliation; early-morning yoga classes are held on the beach daily.

Nosara, Nicoya Peninsula, Costa Rica; 011-506/682-4114; harmonynosara.com; doubles from $$

HACIENDA ZULETA

Imbabura, Ecuador

Potted geraniums line the exterior of Hacienda Zuleta. Opposite: A portrait-lined stairway.

WITH ITS 300 COWS AND 2,000 SHEEP,
Hacienda Zuleta is a working farm that
produces crops (wheat, quinoa, organic
vegetables) in the Ecuadoran Andes, two
hours north of Quito. Purebred Andalu-
sian horses transport guests to the
nearby 800-year-old Caranqui pyramid
mounds, a trout farm, or the resident
condor-rehabilitation project. Each night,
meals at the common table may include
such specials as the inn's famous rice
tart or a heart-of-palm ceviche. On cool
days, guests gather in the sitting room in
front of a fire, where wine is served with
cheese made on the premises.

Angochagua, Imbabura,
Ecuador; 593-6/266-
2182; zuleta.com; doubles
from $$$, including
meals and some activities

A housekeeper at Hacienda San Agustín de Callo. Above: A herd of the estate's llamas.

HACIENDA SAN AGUSTÍN DE CALLO

Cotopaxi, Ecuador

SAN AGUSTÍN DE CALLO HAS DEEP ROOTS AS A lodge. In the foothills of the snowcapped Cotopaxi volcano, 48 miles from Quito, the hacienda sits on the ruins of an Incan *tambo*, a 15th-century inn that once lodged royalty traveling along the Inca Trail. The current owner, Mignon Plaza, inherited the property from her grandfather, Leonidas Plaza, two-time president of Ecuador. The 11 rooms, which are dispersed among three buildings, have wood-beamed ceilings; some also contain brightly frescoed walls and volcano views. Visitors looking to be fully immersed in the inn's ancient history should request one of the three rooms with original Incan walls, which were crafted from precisely carved blocks of stone and then intricately set without mortar. Sections of pre-Columbian masonry are also visible in the two dining rooms, lending a dramatic backdrop for traditional Andean dishes such as quinoa croquettes, or the hacienda's famous *locro,* a potato-and-cheese soup.

Lasso, Cotopaxi, Ecuador; 593-2/290-6157; incahacienda.com; doubles from $$

The main courtyard at Awasi, in the Chilean Atacama Desert.

AWASI

San Pedro de Atacama, Chile

THE ENDLESSLY VARIED ATACAMA DESERT, with its geysers, salt lagoons, volcanoes, and oases, rivals Patagonia as a wilderness destination. Architect Francisco Rencoret and interior decorator Paula Domínguez have built a dream getaway for the adventure-minded. The eight bungalows are made of adobe, stone, and thatch; inside, hardwood and marble floors are set off by Bolivian rugs and wall hangings. Guides are on hand to take guests on excursions such as a bike ride to saline Cejar Pond or a picturesque hike crisscrossing the Vilamar River.

4 Tocapilla, San Pedro de Atacama, Chile; 56-2/233-9641; awasi.cl; doubles from $$$, based on two nights, all-inclusive

A dining room
at Casa Real.

CASA REAL HOTEL

Maipo Valley, Chile

CHILEAN WINE IS FINALLY GARNERING SERIOUS ATTENTION, thanks in part to innovative vintners who are outfitting century-old estates with state-of-the-art technology. Among them: Santa Rita vineyards, 25 miles south of Santiago, in the Maipo Valley. Built in 1880 as the spread's manor house, Casa Real was converted into a hotel in 1996. The 16 rooms have a European glamour, with soaring ceilings and French doors that open onto a grassy courtyard with a stone fountain. Service is attentive and unobtrusive—the fruit basket in each room is perpetually full, the bottled water stocked. A horse-and-cart tour trots guests around the 100-acre manicured grounds, and to the cellars to taste Santa Rita's top-rated Cabernets.

Las Condes, Maipo Valley, Chile; 56-2/821-9966; santarita.com; doubles from $$, including breakfast

LOS LINGUES

Colchagua Valley, Chile

A STAY AT LOS LINGUES is a lesson in regional history. The owner consulted with top architects and historians to restore Chile's oldest hacienda—78 miles south of Santiago, in the Colchagua Valley—to its 1650 colonial style, while adding contemporary luxuries like a pool. Throughout the estate, which comprises a main house and a guesthouse on more than 25,000 acres, rooms are flush with priceless antiques, from 16th-century silver Peruvian fighting cocks to ornate Mapuche necklaces. The plantation's stables shelter its Creole horses, members of a superior breed dating back to the 18th century; they star in daily riding exhibitions held at the on-site rodeo ring. Breakfast is not included, but the elaborate spread of farm-fresh eggs and an entire hock from which to carve slices of ham is worth the extra $24.

Colchagua Valley, Chile; 56-2/431-0510; loslingues.com; doubles from $

The pool at Los Lingues, in the Colchagua Valley.

HOTEL ANTUMALAL

Pucón, Chile

THE CLEAN-LINED AND SLEEK HOTEL ANTUMALAL stands on the edge of Pucón, a backpacker's town with a Wild West feel and a surplus of Internet cafés. Built in the 1950's as an ultramodern lakeside resort, its Bauhaus-influenced architect, Jorge Elton, was inspired by the terraced 13-acre park that surrounds it. The lobby combines tree-slab tables and shaggy fur rugs, formerly cutting-edge elements that now seem decidedly of another era. The 22 rooms blend wood paneling, stone fireplaces, and panoramic windows with views of Lake Villarrica. The natural theme continues in the spa—with treatments such as reflexology and stone massages—and in the restaurant, which serves local river trout, and produce plucked from the property's garden.

Km. 2, Camino Villarrica Pucón, Pucón, Chile; 56-45/441-011; antumalal.com; doubles from $

The Hotel Antumalal is perched above Lake Villarrica, in the Andean foothills. Opposite: The property's Bauhaus-inflected lobby.

CANDELARIA DEL MONTE

San Miguel del Monte, Argentina

A sitting area at the Candelaria del Monte. Opposite: A member of the staff on the patio outside the main house.

CANDELARIA DEL MONTE IS surrounded by nearly 200 acres of
Argentina's famous pampas, vast pasturelands whose striking
topography is broken only by occasional stands of eucalyptus.
The intimate four-bedroom and two-suite colonial property was
a private residence before it opened to guests in 2004, and it
retains a cozy, lived-in feel: black-lacquered antiques, a riot of
chintzes, armchairs with tassel trims. Guests can swim in the
pool, play paddle tennis, or saddle up for one of the hotel's polo
clinics and learn the proper way to wield a mallet. The fruit, eggs,
vegetables, and beef used to prepare the regional dishes are
homegrown, as is the honey, produced at the ranch's own apiary.

San Miguel del Monte,
Argentina; 54-2271/442-431;
candelariadelmonte.com.ar;
doubles from $$, including meals
and most activities

The pool deck at Jungle Bay Resort & Spa, overlooking the Atlantic.

CARIBBEAN+ THE BAHAMAS+ BERMUDA

JADE MOUNTAIN

Soufrière, St. Lucia

St. Lucia's Piton mountains,
seen from an open-air
suite at Jade Mountain.

ST. LUCIA IS FULL OF WATERFALLS AND RAIN FORESTS, a place where birds-of-paradise abound and views of the Gros and Petit Piton mountains evoke the South Pacific. So it's no surprise that new hotels are popping up across the island. Perhaps the boldest play is being made by Jade Mountain, an addition to the Anse Chastanet Resort—a longtime fixture on virtually every Best of the Caribbean list. Located at the highest point of the resort, near the west coast town of Soufrière, the hotel wraps around the hillside, its exterior all curves and rough stone. Inside, each of the 24 suites is unique, but they all share impressive features: infinity pools, 15-foot ceilings, and loftlike architecture—even the raised bathroom is essentially part of one huge space. Walk into the living room and it seems as if you've walked into the Pitons: since there is no fourth wall obscuring the view, it's completely exposed to the elements.

1 Anse Chastanet Rd., Soufrière, St. Lucia; 800/223-1108 or 758/459-4000; jademountainstlucia.com; doubles from $$$$$

DISCOVERY AT MARIGOT BAY

Marigot, St. Lucia

Voile netting drapes a bed in a Discovery at Marigot Bay guest room. Opposite: The Pink Snail lobby bar.

ARRIVE AT THE RECENTLY REINVENTED DISCOVERY at Marigot Bay on St. Lucia's western coast, and the first thing you'll do is a double take. The Pink Snail, its lobby-level champagne lounge and reception area, is a design statement: see-through Ghost chairs by Philippe Starck are arrayed around a glowing pink-resin bar crowned by two huge twinkling chandeliers. The room pays homage to the giant pink snail from 1967's *Dr. Dolittle*, filmed nearby. That's not the only reference to the area's colorful past. The Hurricane Hole bar, once a place where everyone from Sophia Loren to Michael Caine bent their elbows, has been restored to its slightly louche glory, cask-barrel tables and all. But Discovery's overall impact is more au courant than old Caribbean, thanks to the bold, modern interiors of its 57 suites: slate-tiled bathrooms, streamlined shutters, and ebonized desks with tapered, metal-tipped legs. Outside, the lush landscaping makes the buildings look as if they're growing right out of the surrounding rain forest.

Marigot, St. Lucia; 758/458-5300; discoverystlucia.com; doubles from $$

JUNGLE BAY RESORT & SPA

Pointe Mulâtre, Dominica

A Jungle Bay guest cottage sits on stilts, facing the Atlantic. Opposite: One of the resort's simple but elegant sitting rooms.

THE COASTLINE STRETCHING OUT FROM
the Jungle Bay Resort & Spa, a hilly
55-acre retreat at the forefront of
sustainable development in Dominica,
is ragged and green. Owner Sam Raphael
placed each of the 35 private cottages—
staggered along a steep incline facing
the Atlantic—far from its neighbors to
minimize erosion. He also built some
foundations out of rock discarded by local
builders. His altruism extends beyond
the environment: for construction
he hired farmers from the failing banana
industry and trained some to craft
furniture for the guest rooms. The
rough-hewn results make for surroundings that are unrefined, though chicly
so: woven-bamboo fans hang over
dressers handmade from white cedar,
while hammocks in tropical colors sway
above balconies, affording views of
the hazy jungle or the aquamarine sea.

Pointe Mulâtre, Dominica; 767/446-1789;
junglebaydominica.com; doubles from $$

EDEN ROCK HOTEL

Baie de St. Jean, St. Bart's

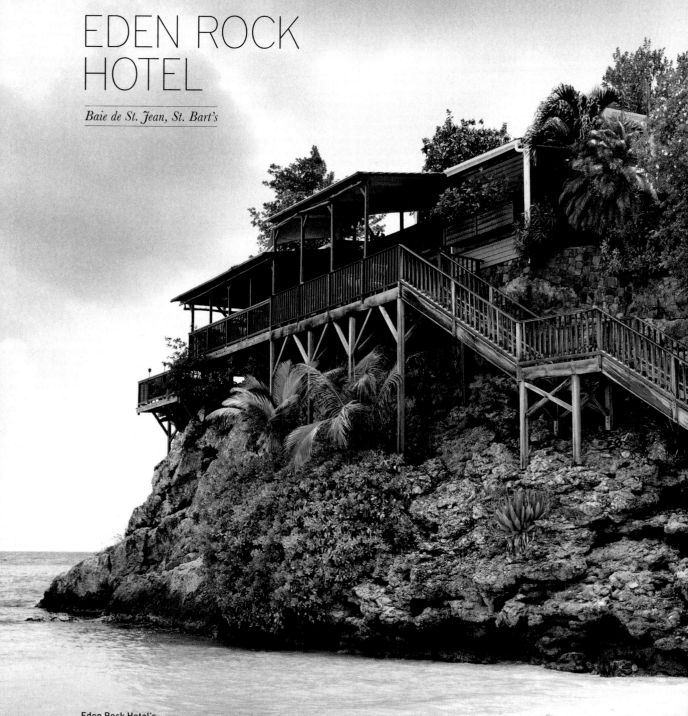

Eden Rock Hotel's restaurant and beach. Opposite: A bedroom in the De Haenen suite.

world's best

WHETHER IT'S THE ROCKY PROMONTORY OF its setting, above the sunbathers on St. Jean beach, or the likelihood of rubbing elbows with Cameron Diaz or Matt Dillon in the Sand Bar, Eden Rock is a perennial epicenter of style on celebrity-studded St. Bart's. The 33 rooms are each different and can include such idiosyncratic details as a rock wall or a Philippe Starck–designed bathroom. The Harbour House and De Haenen suites, which float above the bay, have the best views. With its two bedrooms, the new beachfront Villa Nina is rife with perks: an art gallery with a rotating selection of works on display, a private pool, and even a Mini Cooper to take for a spin.

Baie de St. Jean, St. Bart's; 877/563-7105 or 590-590/297-999; edenrockhotel.com; doubles from $$$$

A guest room's window seat at the Hotel Saint-Barth Isle de France.

HOTEL SAINT-BARTH ISLE DE FRANCE

Baie des Flamands, St. Bart's

world's best

THE 33-ROOM HOTEL SAINT-BARTH ISLE DE FRANCE can't be topped for location—right on Baie des Flamands, the island's longest, widest beach. The 13 oceanfront rooms and suites are the most romantic, with whitewashed interiors, private terraces, and views of the surf. Alternately, 13 cottages hidden among banana and palm trees are perfect for privacy seekers. Distractions include a tennis court, a gym, and a Molton Brown spa. There's also a fashion show every Tuesday evening: guests convene around the pool to watch the attractive staff model bikinis and filmy wraps sold at the boutique. But in the end, the hotel is all about the beach. Even the restaurant makes the most of its location, serving lunches of lobster spring rolls or iced pea soup at tables set in the sand.

MALLIOUHANA HOTEL & SPA

Meads Bay, Anguilla

One of Malliouhana's
two swimming pools.

world's best

WHEN IT OPENED ON THE WEST END OF ANGUILLA IN 1984, the trendsetting 55-room Malliouhana Hotel & Spa helped put the beach-blessed island on the radar of stylish travelers. Today, the hotel continues to set standards for excellence. On a verdant seaside cliff, the suites are vast and richly propped: rattan furniture, dark walnut millwork, and Italian marble bathrooms. At the oceanfront 15,000-square-foot spa, a dedicated staff of 25 provides a wealth of services, from an Ocean Oasis massage employing marine mud to a one-on-one game of basketball with a personal trainer. The Michelin-starred restaurant, named for its chef, Michel Rostang, is just as well-equipped. Accompaniment for such dishes as lobster ravioli in coconut milk or gingerbread-crusted veal can be found in the wine cellar, known for its stock of 25,000 bottles.

Meads Bay, Anguilla; 800/835-0796 or 264/497-6111; malliouhana.com; doubles from $$$$

An arbor shades a whirlpool at Tortuga Bay. Opposite, top and bottom: The sitting area of a newly renovated Puntacana casita; the resort's palm-lined beach.

PUNTACANA RESORT & CLUB

Punta Cana, Dominican Republic

BUILT IN 1971, PUNTACANA WAS THE FIRST
resort development on the untouched
east coast of the Dominican Republic.
Since then, its shores have seen tremen-
dous growth, and so has the property—
from its inception as a tiny 10-villa hotel to
a sprawling complex that caters to every
taste. These days, there's a newly opened
Six Senses spa, a 70-slip marina, a pair
of Tom Fazio– and P. B. Dye–designed
golf courses, nine restaurants, seven bars,
a biodiversity center, and a 1,500-acre
nature preserve. The main hotel's beachfront casitas were recently given a makeover. Khaki-hued walls, dark wicker furniture, and throw pillows in graphic botanical
prints pack a tropical punch. And the
new Tortuga Bay—an exclusive 32-suite
resort-within-a-resort designed by part-
time resident Oscar de la Renta—has been
a hit with boldface names (Harrison Ford
and Calista Flockhart among them). Each
of the villas has a fully stocked kitchen,
an oversize coralline stone bathroom, a
clean Caribbean aesthetic, and a personal
golf cart for exploring.

Punta Cana, Dominican Republic; 888/442-2262
or 809/959-2262; puntacana.com; doubles from $$;
doubles at Tortuga Bay from $$$$

THE COVE AT ATLANTIS

Paradise Island, Bahamas

The lobby at the Cove.
Opposite: The hotel's
main pool, surrounded
by private cabanas.

AT THE 2,900-ROOM ATLANTIS RESORT, HOTELIER Sol Kerzner has created a seductive set of alternate realities: a lagoon stocked with sharks, an underground aquarium, and an opulent Royal Towers lobby, whose tall columns seem to have been borrowed not from the Parthenon but from a buttercream-frosted cake. When he introduced the 600-suite Cove, a smaller hotel incorporated into the larger complex, Kerzner exercised more restraint than usual. The Cove is designed to attract exactly the sort of sophisticates who would snub Atlantis proper. All coral pink with oddball turrets from the outside, it fits in with the overstatement of the rest of the property. But here, the porte cochère is designed not as a gateway to a fish tank–fantasy world but as a framing device for a view of the actual ocean. Inside, the idea is modern chic à la Las Vegas, courtesy of interior designers Jeffrey Beers and David Rockwell. The Cove's palette is controlled cool: lots of teak, iridescent mother-of-pearl, and quiet touches like the perforated copper siding along the open kitchen at Mesa Grill. In the light-filled rooms, even the bathtubs have spectacular water vistas.

1 Casino Dr., Paradise Island, The Bahamas; 877/268-3847 or 954/809-2100; atlantis.com; doubles from $$$

KAMALAME CAY

Kamalame Cay, Bahamas

THE SHORT FERRY RIDE FROM NEIGHBORING ANDROS reveals nothing of this private 96-acre barrier island but thick stands of mangrove trees. Secluded Kamalame Cay is the perfect stage for an updated Robinson Crusoe fantasy. There are no televisions in the 19 villas, but latter-day castaways can luxuriate in quarters that combine Indonesian furniture, Oriental carpets, and muslin-draped French doors. It's as if you've been shipwrecked with a staff dedicated to your every desire, whether it's a snorkeling trip to the nearby reef, dinner on the three-mile-long beach, or a coffee body scrub at the spa, which hovers on stilts above the sea.

Kamalame Cay, The Bahamas; 800/790-7971 or 242/368-6281; kamalame.com; doubles from $$$$

Kamalame Cay's
dining room. Opposite:
The Cottage suite,
50 feet from the beach.

ELBOW BEACH

Paget Parish, Bermuda

IN THE NEXT FEW YEARS, WHEN THE LAST stroke of clotted cream–colored paint is applied to the grand dowager duchess of Bermuda resorts, when the last lacy fan of dried marine algae is mounted in a box frame and hung, Elbow Beach will be rebranded as a Mandarin Oriental resort. (The company currently holds only the management contract.) Guests can already see the transformation in the 235 guest rooms and the spa. Scuttled once and for all are the juicy pinks and greens and the hothouse florals. In place of that endearing look is a soothing and serene palette, with sharp tailored furniture in blond wood and natural wicker. The spa, with its bamboo floors, hand-carved granite tubs, and river-rock showers, is a page from the same stylish book.

60 S. Shore Rd., Paget Parish, Bermuda; 800/526-6566 or 441/236-3535; mandarinoriental.com; doubles from $$

The balcony of an Elbow Beach Spa suite.

A dining room in Waterloo House's ABS suite. Right: The infinity pool of a Cambridge Beaches suite.

WATERLOO HOUSE

Hamilton, Bermuda

ON PAPER, IT'S A RECIPE FOR FAILURE: A BERMUDIAN resort without a beach—who would go? But the 30-room Waterloo pulls it off, trumping geography with sophistication and refinement. The 19th-century manor house and its cottages rule from a terraced roost on Hamilton Harbour. The atmosphere is VVB (Very Very British), happily meaning lots of GEF (Good English Furniture), like mahogany antiques and rose-covered upholstery. Proximity to the island's financial district makes it a hit among business travelers, but if you prefer play over work, hop a taxi: guests have full privileges at the nearby Coral Beach & Tennis Club, a staid enterprise dedicated to leisurely pursuits. Croquet, anyone?

100 Pitts Bay Rd., Hamilton, Pembroke Parish, Bermuda; 800/468-4100 or 441/295-4480; waterloohouse.com; doubles from $$

CAMBRIDGE BEACHES

Sandys Parish, Bermuda

THE 94-ROOM CAMBRIDGE BEACHES MAY BE THE preppiest, most conservative place on the island (you'd swear you were at a country club), but the resort, on 30 acres of Bermuda's remote west end, does think outside the box: it's the only one that has accommodations with dedicated pools. Each of the three freestanding new suites overlooks the Atlantic and includes a bedroom, a sitting room, a dressing room, a whirlpool tub set before a picture window, a six-head shower stall with an independent sound system—plus an infinity-edge plunge pool. Coffered ceilings, cutting-garden chintz, and gourd lamps on mahogany night tables assure the old guard that Cambridge hasn't gone off the deep end.

30 Kings Point, Sandys Parish, Bermuda; 800/468-7300 or 441/234-0331; cambridgebeaches.com; doubles from $$, including breakfast

88

EUROPE

Villa Pisani, surrounded by 19th-century gardens, in Italy's Veneto region.

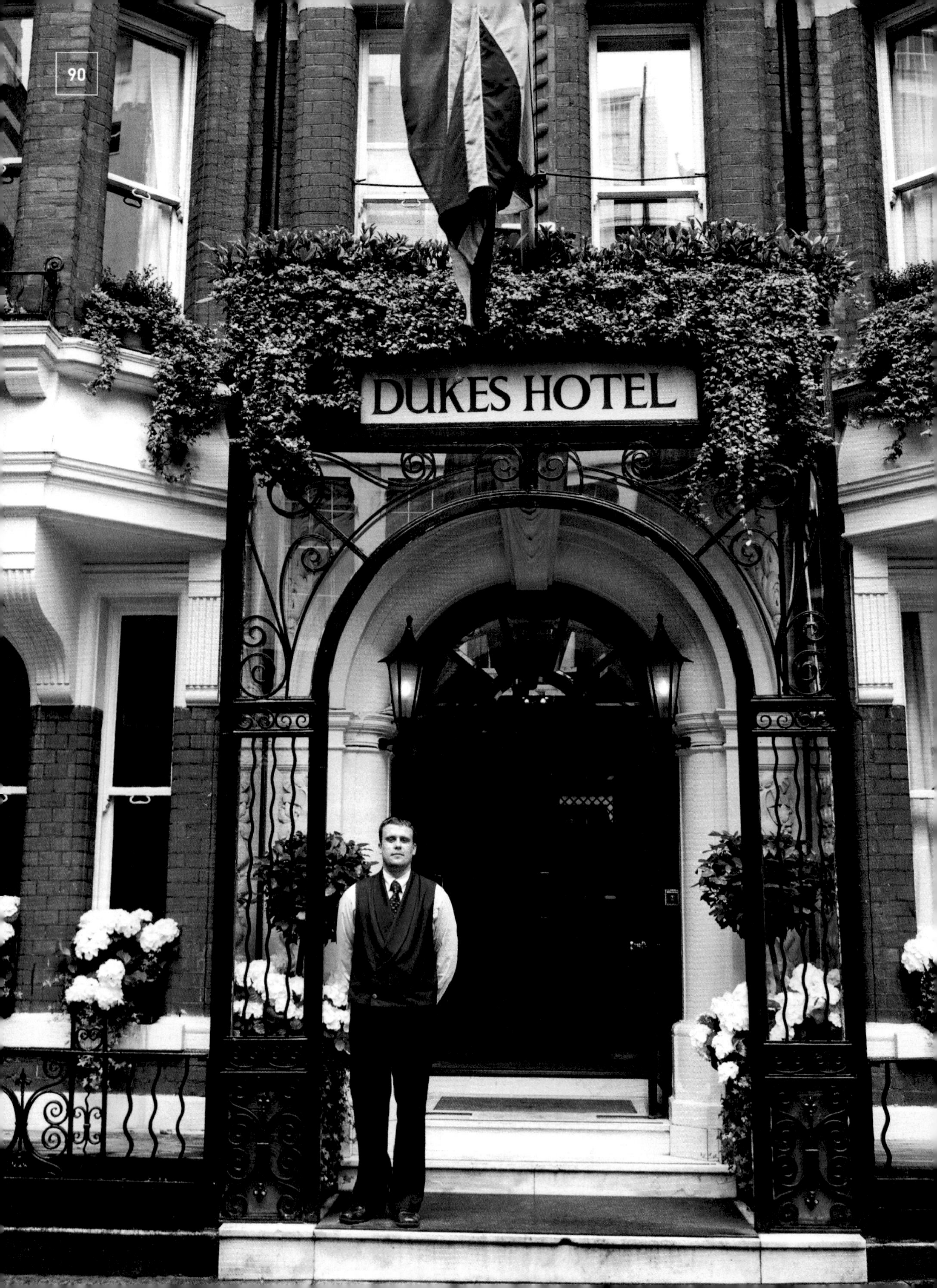
DUKES HOTEL

Right: Portraits and prints in the bar at Dukes Hotel in London. Below: A newly renovated guest room. Opposite: A bellman on the front steps of the hotel.

DUKES HOTEL

London, England

SINCE 1908, DUKES HAS OCCUPIED A PAIR of discreet town houses on a London cul-de-sac just blocks from Green Park and Clarence House. Last spring, the down-at-the-heels classic was reinvented by Gordon Campbell Gray and Mary Fox Linton, the duo responsible for nearby One Aldwych, as well as Carlisle Bay in Antigua. Linton has stripped away faded flourishes (chintz bedskirts, pub-green carpets), adding fresh linen upholstery and a calm limestone-tiled foyer. All 90 rooms have a soothing, predominantly blue-and-cream palette and granite baths. Still, Dukes retains a certain grandeur, evidenced in polished mahogany doors, a handsome iron central staircase, real keys, and oil paintings in the formal spaces. Another winning touch: hot buttered crumpets served in the drawing room. Best of all, the welcoming staff puts on zero airs, despite the posh address.

St. James's Place, London, England; 800/525-4800 or 44-20/7491-4840; dukeshotel.com; doubles from $$$

Above, left: A corner of the revamped InterContinental London Park Lane's lobby. Above: The hotel's façade.

INTERCONTINENTAL LONDON PARK LANE

London, England

CHANGE HAS COME TO THE INTERCONTINENTAL LONDON PARK LANE. The hotel's famously posh location—between Hyde and Green parks, with regal views of Buckingham Palace—is now matched by its interiors. The property recently emerged from a $118 million makeover, with rooms swathed in damask and linen. In one loftlike suite, floor-to-ceiling windows frame a panorama that includes the queen's residence and Wellington Arch. The hot new London design firm J2 added dramatic touches to the knockout lobby, such as cascading chandeliers that drip like icicles.

One Hamilton Place, Park Lane, London, England; 800/327-0200 or 44-20/7409-3131; intercontinental.com; doubles from $$

SLOANE SQUARE

London, England

A room at London's Sloane Square hotel.

SET ON THE HISTORIC CHELSEA PARK THAT gives the property its name, the revamped 102-room Sloane Square hotel is a pared-down yet polished gem imbued with traditional British flair. Floral wallpaper by Neisha Crossland and Scottish-tartan wool bedspreads set the mood in the comfortable rooms. And personal details abound: 10 rooms have oversize beds for tall guests, and all are equipped with blackout shades, ensuring the most luxurious amenity of all—a good night's sleep.

Sloane Square, London, England; 44-20/7896-9988; sloanesquarehotel.co.uk; doubles from $$

GLENAPP CASTLE

Ballantrae, Scotland

The Victorian-era Glenapp Castle, in the Scottish countryside.

THE 90-MINUTE DRIVE FROM GLASGOW to the 17-room Glenapp Castle unfolds like the opening credits of a romance movie, with moorland glens and tumbled, lichen-speckled citadels. Just outside Ballantrae, a tree-lined lane leads to the 19th-century pink-sandstone manor, looking out on the Irish Sea from a crest above the rocky shore. Glenapp has all the features a castle lover craves: there is a hidden spiral staircase, walled gardens, and a tartan-bedecked library where steaming cups of Earl Grey tea and raisin scones are served. In the marigold-yellow Earl of Orkney bedroom, one of the largest Master rooms, the silk curtains, filigreed fire grate, and plump damask sofa are regal—and close-up ready.

Ballantrae, Scotland; 800/735-2478 or 44-1465/831-212; glenappcastle.com; doubles from $$$$, including breakfast and dinner

Left: Inside the Drawing Room, near Builth Wells, Wales. Below: The inn's terrace.

DRAWING ROOM

Builth Wells, Wales

A NUMBER OF WELSH COUNTRY INNS ARE beginning to lure visitors with sophisticated food that rivals the quality of the bucolic views. Londoners are willing to drive almost four hours to reach the Drawing Room, a five-table restaurant and three-room hotel near the historic market town of Builth Wells. The inn, with antique pine furniture, fireplaces, and a perfectly tended garden, inhabits a 1725 Georgian house. Chefs Melanie and Colin Dawson prepare Cardigan Bay crab salad with prawns, avocado, caviar, and mustard mayonnaise for dinner, and favorites such as duck eggs with wild mushrooms at breakfast. All ingredients are locally sourced—except for the *beurre français*, which the Dawsons adopted only after much deliberation.

Cwmbach, Builth Wells, Powys, Wales; 44-198/255-2493; the-drawing-room.co.uk; doubles from $$, including breakfast and dinner

LLYS MEDDYG

Newport, Wales

The dining room, with antique Pembroke tables, at Llys Meddyg.

YOUNG WELSH COUPLE ED AND LOUISE SYKES RETURNED to their homeland after a seven-year stint in London to transform a former carriage house and stable in the coastal town of Newport into a shabby-chic six-room inn and restaurant. In the antiques-filled lounge, contemporary art lines the walls, and guest rooms, spread out between the two buildings, have an urbane palette, with chunky reclaimed-wood headboards and tall Georgian windows. At the restaurant, chef Davide Daltoe's seasonal dishes— Preseli lamb cutlets in a delicate rosemary *jus*, a flavorful spiced pumpkin soup—are a subtle triumph.

Newport, Pembrokeshire, Wales;
44-1239/820-008; llysmeddyg.com;
doubles from $, including breakfast

The Bell at Skenfrith, in Wales. Right: A Welsh-oak bed in one of the guest rooms.

BELL AT SKENFRITH

Skenfrith, Wales

THIS 17TH-CENTURY INN ABOUT 160 MILES NORTHWEST of London was refurbished in 2001, but it still retains an inviting, lived-in feel. Wing chairs and rich, cream-colored walls add warmth to the cool flagstone floors of the main sitting room, and the eight guest rooms have all the comforts you'd expect from a Welsh country residence (wool blankets, mahogany antiques). In the restaurant, chef David Hill updates classic Welsh dishes—roasted pork tenderloin with black pudding and mushroom foam—but desserts such as berry crumble and trifle remain comfortingly traditional.

Skenfrith, Monmouthshire, Wales; 44-160/075-0235; skenfrith.co.uk; doubles from $, including breakfast

The corridor lobby
of the Ritz Paris.
Opposite, top:
The Coco Chanel
suite. Opposite,
below: Inside the
hotel's entrance.

RITZ
PARIS

Paris, France

FOR THE PAST 110 YEARS, THE identity of the Ritz Paris, on the Place Vendôme, has been embedded in niceties so subtle, they're felt rather than noticed: bedside command centers for summoning a waiter, sheets laundered in *savon de Marseille.* But in the face of the most acute competition in its long history, the ultimate grand hotel has introduced a potent cocktail of fresh services, gadgets, indulgences, and enticements. Decorator Pierre-Yves Rochon has freshened guest rooms with elegant touches such as upholstered-and-gilded beds fit for a dauphin. New chapters in the hotel's history are being written with an all-organic room service menu. Purists will still find indelibly Ritz elements: the long corridor lobby, with its few thronelike chairs and towering windows dressed in swags and jabots; the gallery of 89 retail vitrines. And what could be more Ritz than the delivery of your dinner check, under the cloudscape ceiling of L'Espadon restaurant, 60 seconds after it is requested—just as the service handbook requires?

15 Place Vendôme, 1st Arr., Paris, France; 33-1/43-16-30-30; ritzparis.com; doubles from $$$$

A suspended bed at the Five Hotel

FIVE HOTEL

Paris, France

LOCATED IN THE LATIN QUARTER near the small cafés and open-air market of busy Rue Mouffetard, the Five Hotel aims to cater to every sense (hence its name). The 24 small but well-planned rooms have clever details such as adjustable colored lighting and a menu of air fragrances. Doubles are known as Glimmering Superiors for the tiny fiber-optic stars adorning the ceilings of canopy beds; and throughout, you'll find hallways paneled in red leather and illuminated glass desks. The one sense given short shrift is hearing; rooms are blissfully quiet, thanks to double-glazed windows.

3 Rue Flatters, 5th Arr., Paris, France; 33-1/43-31-74-21; thefivehotel.com; doubles from $

HÔTEL FOUQUET'S BARRIÈRE

Paris, France

THE LUCIEN BARRIÈRE GROUP BEHIND THE LEGENDARY palace hotels the Majestic, in Cannes, and Deauville's Normandy recently raised the stakes in five-star Paris with Hôtel Fouquet's Barrière, a 107-room property on the Champs-Élysées. Even the basic rooms have flat-screen TV's encased in sharkskin, separate dressing areas, and butler service. Public areas are no less lavish: embroidered leather covers lobby walls, and hundreds of silver-dipped tree branches decorate the terrace. Service aims yet higher—guests are e-mailed a two-page questionnaire addressing mini-bar, pillow, and ambient-music preferences in advance of their stay.

46 Ave. George V, 8th Arr., Paris, France; 800/223-6800 or 33-1/40-69-60-00; fouquets-barriere.com; doubles from $$$$$

The indoor pool at the U Spa in the Hôtel Fouquet's Barrière.

LE CANARD A TROIS PATTES

Dordogne, France

BELGIANS ARMAND VAN LIERDE AND GREET DECREUS
are B&B owners from heaven: discreet, cultivated,
and laissez-faire. They also demonstrate great
reductionist style. Inside Le Canard a Trois Pattes,
their 15th-century farmhouse in France's Dordogne
region, chairs made of rigid polyurethane foam
are pulled up to an old refectory table. One of the five
guest rooms has a mattress that floats in the
middle of the room; the only other furnishings are a
butterfly chair; a flaking folding park chair; and
a huge ottoman in chocolate cowhide. The dishes
Decreus coaxes from her retro Smeg fridge and
butter-yellow Aga stove are no less simple:
grilled eggplant involtini piped with goat cheese,
cherry-tomato risotto, a cinnamony apple tart.

Le Castanet, Tamniès, Dordogne, France; 33-5/53-59-13-85; troispattes.com; doubles from $$, including breakfast

The pool and 15th-century farmhouse, with a modern addition, at Le Canard a Trois Pattes. Opposite: The B&B's Hirondelle room.

HOTEL-RESTAURANT BRAS

Laguiole, France

The glass-encased dining
room of Hotel-Restaurant Bras.

TEN MINUTES UP THE ROAD FROM LAGUIOLE, a mountainous town in the sparsely populated département of Aveyron, is Hotel-Restaurant Bras, a large, luminous, and sparely portioned property with sculptural beige wicker armchairs and huge beds covered in sheets that are indescribably fine. The main attraction, however, is the Michelin three-starred Restaurant Bras, a futuristic metal-and-glass structure poised on an immense carpet of vegetation. Father-son team Michel and Sébastien Bras prepare signature dishes: a first course of *gargouillou*, a sautéed medley of more than 50 vegetables that contrasts a complex preparation with an exquisitely simple presentation. At lunch, light fills the restaurant, which is cantilevered over the plateau of Aubrac, giving diners the impression they are in a spaceship hovering above the countryside.

Rte. de l'Aubrac, Laguiole, France; 800/735-2478 or 33-5/65-51-18-20; michel-bras.fr; doubles from $$

JARDINS SECRETS

Nîmes, France

DESPITE BEING IN DOWNTOWN NÎMES, JARDINS SECRETS feels like a romantic rural refuge, with 14 guest rooms and a small swimming pool shaded by orange and olive trees hidden behind a pink façade. Antiques, bowls of freshly snipped roses, and silk-curtained bathing alcoves with freestanding rolltop tubs make this one of the most desirable addresses west of the Rhône. It's an ideal base for touring the area's ruins: a first-century A.D. amphitheater and the impressive temple La Maison Carrée are just a short stroll away.

3 Rue Gaston Maruejols, Nîmes, France; 33-4/66-84-82-64; jardinssecrets.net; doubles from $$

The Grisailles room at Jardins Secrets.

Right: The courtyard at
L'Ange et L'Eléphant.
Below: Indian doors framing
the hotel's entrance.

L'ANGE ET L'ELÉPHANT

Maussane les Alpilles, France

HISTORICALLY, PROVINCIAL MAISONS D'HÔTES
are a lot of things—deliciously louche,
impossibly cute, poignantly decrepit—but
rarely are they scene-y. L'Ange et l'Eléphant
is the salutary exception, an all-in-one inn,
restaurant, tea salon, and boutique. The
guesthouse, in a massive 18th-century
staging post, is a lovely three-minute walk
from the town's main square. Inside,
the two-room Franco-Indo-Arabic inn is
decorated with a mix of disparate trans-
porting elements: tole cacti, cedar panels
of lacy latticed moucharaby, and vintage
Coca-Cola picnic coolers. The 750-square-
foot suite has a salon that drifts into an
open kitchen, and a terrace overlooking
the courtyard below.

9 Rue de la Reine Jeanne, Maussane les Alpilles, France;
33-4/90-54-18-34; elephange.com; doubles from $

LE MANOIR DE L'ETANG

Mougins, France

The lobby of
Le Manoir
de L'Etang.

AFTER BUYING LE MANOIR DE L'ETANG FROM the family who had owned it for more than 50 years, Camilla Richards gave it a modern update, filling the ivy-covered Côte d'Azur villa with eclectic touches. In the 20 rooms, spread among four buildings, abstract prints adorn the walls and salvaged doors form headboards on beds covered with vibrantly hued linen pillows. Outside, guests lounge by the pool or stroll around the property's lotus flower–filled lake. The restaurant, Il Lago, serving dishes such as gnocchi with mint, is a destination in its own right.

66 Allee du Manoir, Mougins, France;
33-4/92-28-36-00; manoir-de-letang.com;
doubles from $$

The courtyard at the Dylan, in Amsterdam.

THE DYLAN

Amsterdam, The Netherlands

384 Keizersgracht, Amsterdam, The Netherlands;
31-20/530-2010; dylanamsterdam.com;
doubles from $$$

ON THE SITE OF AMSTERDAM'S FIRST THEATER IN AN 18th-century building, the Dylan is making a design statement, thanks to its inimitable interiors by Anouska Hempel. The 41 rooms alternate between Flemish austerity and Asian opulence. In the Loft suite, old-fashioned screens and low-slung sofas are done in restrained shades of white, cream, and oatmeal; conversely, the La Carmona suite is decorated with a Chinese chest and orange-and-brown-striped walls. Downstairs, the bar's gold-leaf walls literally glow from a 2006 refurbishment by Dutch design firm FG stijl. There, Dries Van Noten–clad locals lounge on acid-green leather chairs, taking in the show.

The atrium at the Sofitel Berlin
Gendarmenmarkt, where breakfast
is served. Opposite, from left:
The Aigner bar; a suite at the hotel.

SOFITEL BERLIN GENDARMENMARKT

Berlin, Germany

THE SOFITEL BERLIN GENDARMENMARKT'S UNASSUMING façade gets lost amid the 18th- and 19th-century pomp of Mitte, the historic center of Berlin. But once you enter the marble-and-glass lobby, the hotel reveals itself as a sleek alternative to the gilded palaces off Unter den Linden. The 92 rooms and suites manage a sharp spareness that doesn't skimp on luxury: beds are piled with thick eiderdown duvets, and the monochrome bathrooms are amply sized; many have both bathtubs and shower stalls. In some of the rooms, balconies take full advantage of the surrounding neighborhood's architectural splendor, affording views of the colonnaded cupola of the Französischer Dom.

50–52 Charlottenstrasse, Berlin, Germany; 800/763-4835 or 49-30/203-750; sofitel.com; doubles from $$

The lobby of the Hotel de Rome.

HOTEL DE ROME

Berlin, Germany

THE ROCCO FORTE GROUP TYPICALLY MAKES MAGIC out of run-down but exquisitely situated properties, like Brown's Hotel in London and the Hotel de Russie in Rome. Their latest accomplishment: Hotel de Rome, set in Berlin's former Dresdner Bank. Interior designer Tommaso Ziffer filled the lobby with dark velvet upholstered furniture and Romanesque vases. The 146 rooms and suites combine tufted linen headboards, wood-paneled walls, and coordinating sofas and chairs in muted color schemes. Onetime bank vaults now house a black granite–clad spa.

37 Behrenstrasse, Berlin, Germany; 888/667-9477 or 49-30/460-6090; hotelderome.com; doubles from $$

VIETNAMONAMOUR

Milan, Italy

IN MILAN'S RESIDENTIAL CITTÀ STUDI NEIGHBORHOOD, fashion and furnishings designer Christiane Blanchet has spruced up a 1903 villa with her signature Indochine aesthetic. The four rooms at this affordable gem showcase artisan-crafted Vietnamese furniture and hand-stitched silk quilts; brick walls are set off with dusky ocher or pink plaster and graphic floral wallpaper. The sliver of a restaurant further mines geographical influences with contemporary Southeast Asian cuisine—*pho* and spring rolls share the menu with tamarind-glazed lamb. The space overlooks a garden and glows with lanterns shaped like flower buds.

7 Via Alessandro Pestalozza, Milan, Italy; 39-02/7063-4614; vietnamonamour.com; doubles from $, including breakfast

A guest room at Milan's Vietnamonamour.

Left: The cocktail bar at Nhow. Below: A guest room.

NHOW

Milan, Italy

IN THE BUZZING TORTONA AREA OF ITALY'S industrial capital, Matteo Thun's 249-room Nhow hotel—housed in a former factory— features a revolving showcase of contemporary art and furniture from Edra, Kartell, and other all-star design companies. There are witty, irreverent touches everywhere, from the graffiti-tagged guest-room doors to the chandelier/sculpture in the restaurant, which mimics the form of a giant iridescent orchid. Art is front and center throughout: one reaches reception via a concrete-columned tunnel where projections and temporary exhibitions are installed, and the hotel maintains a separate gallery Web site dedicated to the works—by the likes of David LaChapelle and Hans Hartung—on display in its halls.

35 Via Tortona, Milan, Italy; 39-02/489-8861; nhow-hotels.com; doubles from $$$$

VILLA TIBOLDI

Piedmont, Italy

IN 1996, WINEMAKERS ROBERTO AND PATRIZIA Damonte bought a dilapidated 18th-century villa near Alba, in Italy's Piedmont region. By 2003, they'd transformed it into Villa Tiboldi, a lovely hotel with a well-placed pool looking out on a steep hill of vineyards. The 10 rooms, some with ceiling murals, are stocked with provincial furniture and curtains, and bed linens in an array of patterned fabrics. With each morning's fog, Patrizia arrives bearing freshly laid eggs that she prepares for breakfast, and one by one guests throw open the shutters to the day; at lunchtime, dishes such as roasted squab with mustard and a green-tomato marmalade are served on the terrace.

127 Case Sparse Tiboldi, Canale, Piedmont, Italy; 39-0173/970-388; villatiboldi.it; doubles from $

The pool at Villa Tiboldi, with a view of the hotel's vineyard.

HOTEL VILLA CIPRIANI

Asolo, Italy

Hotel Villa Cipriani, at a bend in Via Canova in the historic center of Asolo.

ASOLO HAS A LOT TO CROW ABOUT: the medieval town in the Dolomite foothills has a Roman past, arcaded streets, and a lively café life. You can walk to everything from the Hotel Villa Cipriani, a country house once owned by Robert Browning, later managed by Giuseppe Cipriani, and finally acquired by Starwood. Hidden behind a high wall, the hotel's 31 rooms combine high wood-beamed ceilings, pedigreed antiques, and tall windows dressed in pom-pom–trimmed curtains framing views of landscapes that will put you in mind of a Titian painting.

298 Via Canova, Asolo, Italy; 800/325-3535 or 39-0423/523-411; starwoodhotels.com; doubles from $$

Villa Pisani's Red Room. Right: The formal dining room at Ca' Zen.

VILLA PISANI

Vescovana, Italy

WISTFUL FOR AN ERA WHEN BEING WELL-BORN, LANDED, and Italian meant a life of little exertion, Mariella Bolognesi Scalabrin runs the eight-room Villa Pisani with chic remove. The 1552 estate sits unbothered 15 miles south of Padua in a country setting. Curtains of vines sweep the grounds, and breakfast is served in the 19th-century garden, which is seen to best advantage from the guest rooms, especially Irina, which is laden with needlepoint, velvet, and lace, and has enchanting allegorical frescoes by Andrea Palladio's collaborator Zelotti.

19-25 Via Roma, Vescovana, Italy; 39-0425/920-016; villapisani.it; doubles from $

CA' ZEN

Taglio di Po, Italy

CA' ZEN, IN THE PARCO REGIONALE DEL DELTA PO— a 70,000-acre puzzle of tidal flats and swamps— was built in the 18th century as a shooting lodge and later ballooned into a *palazzina*. Seven rooms and a cottage contain hourglass slipper chairs, flouncy dressing tables, and blackamoors, all of which were handed down to owner Elaine Avanzo Westropp Bennet's late husband. Daughter Maria Adelaide is also part of the family business, and will offer to serve your breakfast at a table overlooking the estate's stunning park.

Taglio di Po, Italy; 39-0426/346-469; tenutacazen.it; doubles from $, including breakfast

Left: The bar at the Duomo Hotel. Below: A window above a guest-room bed looks into the bathroom. Opposite: Part of the lobby, with a portion of the doughnut-shaped front desk.

DUOMO HOTEL

Rimini, Italy

EYEBROWS WERE RAISED WHEN LONDON-based designer Ron Arad, known for his sinuous metal furniture, announced plans for a hotel in the Italian seaside resort of Rimini, an hour east of Bologna on the Adriatic coast. The town is no design destination, and many considered it a strange spot for some of Arad's latest work. But his 43-room property, with intergalactic shapes in metal, wood, and Corian, represents the thrill of the future. Standards are 270 square feet and sparsely furnished; in each, a circular window in the wall behind the bed looks into the bathroom (Venetian blinds allow for privacy). Most successful is the lobby bar, where Arad's steel Kompass tables are flanked by his cream Ripple chairs. It's all a seductive celebration of form over function, and it dazzles.

28 Via G. Bruno, Rimini, Italy; 39-05/412-4215; duomohotel.com; doubles from $$

The patio at Villa Bordoni, as seen from the hotel's garden.

VILLA BORDONI

Greve in Chianti, Italy

31–32 Via San Cresci, Greve in Chianti, Italy; 39-055/884-0004; villabordoni.it; doubles from $$, including breakfast

IN 2002, TRANSPLANTED SCOTTISH RESTAURATEURS David and Catherine Gardner discovered a ruin in Chianti and turned it into the wisteria-covered Villa Bordoni. The first-time hoteliers hired local interior designer Riccardo Barthel, who juxtaposed wood-paneled ceilings and antique bathroom tiles with witty touches like straw curtain tassels and a chicken-coop wall hanging. But it's the whimsically decorated restaurant (frescoes feature thistles and vines) that's the Gardners' pride and joy. Chef Francesco Fineo reinterprets classic local ingredients—squab is paired with mashed celeriac and a grape-must reduction—while remaining true to traditional dishes such as *bistecca alla fiorentina*.

A sitting room at the Villa Spalletti Trivelli, hung with 16th-century tapestries.

VILLA SPALLETTI TRIVELLI

Rome, Italy

4 Via Piacenza, Rome, Italy; 39-06/4890-7934; doubles from $$$$$, including breakfast

LOCATED ON ROME'S QUIRINAL HILL, JUST ABOVE THE Imperial Forum, the Villa Spalletti Trivelli glows from a recent $7 million restoration. Up until 1998 the hotel was the private home of the Spalletti Trivelli family (titled since 1667), and many of the furnishings are heirlooms: rare Piranesi prints hang in hallways, the Pineider correspondence paper bears the clan's coat of arms, and 15-foot tapestries line the walls. Upstairs, rooms are no less elegant, with color-coordinated damasks on the armchairs and fine wooden tables mixed with Lucite ones. All of this, plus a capable staff, makes good on the hotel's proclaimed mandate: affording guests the opportunity to live like a nobleman—at least for a night.

Portrait Suites' rooftop terrace, with a view of the Spanish Steps. Right: The lounge at the Inn at the Roman Forum.

PORTRAIT SUITES

Rome, Italy

ROME'S FOUR-STORY PORTRAIT SUITES, CENTRALLY located near the Spanish Steps, is part of the Lungarno Hotels group, owned by the Ferragamo family. And thanks to interior designer Michele Bönan, it's a chic and sexy urban retreat. Walls are black-stained French oak, white-marble bathrooms have gunmetal-gray floors, and ice-blue flannel chairs are placed in front of logo-dotted, chartreuse-lined silk curtains. The roof terrace is all teak furniture and carefully clipped potted boxwoods—a perfect foil for the Baroque splendor it overlooks.

23 Via Bocca di Leone, Rome, Italy; 39-06/6938-0742; lungarnohotels.com; doubles from $$$, including breakfast

INN AT THE ROMAN FORUM

Rome, Italy

THE IVY-DRAPED PALAZZO HOUSING THE INN AT THE Roman Forum—near Via Nazionale at the cross-roads of the ancient capital—has flawless bones. A regal marble staircase spirals up four floors from the reception area to a cozy lounge, and its 12 rooms are spacious, with high coffered ceilings and beautifully inlaid parquet floors. Furnishings blend the old (canopied iron beds) and the new (rain showers, granite sinks). But modern touches don't distract from the hotel's history: the 17th-century building stands on a 2,000-year-old crypt, accessed via a glass door behind the concierge desk.

30 Via degli Ibernesi, Rome, Italy; 39-06/6919-0970; doubles from $$$, including breakfast

LA ROSA DEI VENTI

Amalfi Coast, Italy

LONG A JET-SET PLAYGROUND, Italy's Amalfi Coast is still accessible, thanks to a handful of affordable hotels that includes La Rosa dei Venti. On a cliff in Positano, La Rosa's seven rooms are furnished simply, with a mix of painted wooden beds and chairs, wall-mounted Madonnas and putti, and bright-hued Vietri ceramic floor tiles. *Mezzogiorno* sunshine floods through French doors— all of which have Mediterranean views. And just a few yards from the inn's entrance, 400-odd steps lead straight to the see-and-be-seen Fornillo beach.

40 Via Fornillo, Positano, Italy; 39-089/875-252; larosadeiventi.net; doubles from $, including breakfast

The terrace of La Rosa dei Venti's Libeccio Room, looking out on the Mediterranean Sea.

CAOL ISHKA HOTEL

Sicily, Italy

CAOL ISHKA, GAELIC FOR "SOUND OF WATER," sits on the bucolic Anapo River just outside the Sicilian town of Ortigia. The young owners, Emanuela Marino and Gareth Shaughnessy, have retained the skeletons of original farm buildings but redesigned their interiors to make 10 rustically soigné rooms with wooden roofs, lavish showers, and stylish Italian lighting and fixtures. You can get Wi-Fi out on the veranda, ringed by papyrus and stands of bamboo, or sit by the river and watch the rowers go by in their shells.

Via Elorina, Contrada Pantanelli, Siracusa, Italy; 866/376-7831 or 39-0931/69057; caolishka.com; doubles from $$

A view of the grounds at
Sicily's Caol Ishka Hotel, as seen
from its infinity pool.

CASA TALÌA

Sicily, Italy

SEEN FROM THE GARDEN OF CASA TALÌA, the village of Modica looks dreamlike, with labyrinthine passageways swirling down the steep sides of a ravine. Seven years ago, Milanese architects Viviana Haddad and Marco Giunta acquired five adjacent houses in what was once a ghetto to create the bed-and-breakfast, bringing an urban sensibility to the ancient stones. They have taken great care in choosing simple but beautiful materials—lace coverlets, pressed-iron beds, and bamboo ceilings. Thanks to wireless Internet, Giunta runs his design business from underneath their fig tree, where breakfast is also served, and the homemade jam—made from Pachino tomatoes with flesh that looks molten—tastes like the sun.

1/9 Via Exaudinos, Modica, Italy; 39-0932/752-075; casatalia.com; doubles from $, including breakfast

The Il Mediterraneo room at Casa Talìa.
Opposite: The view of Modica from the hotel's garden.

ROOM MATE ALICIA

Madrid, Spain

2 Calle Prado, Madrid, Spain;
34/91-389-6095; room-matehotels.com;
doubles from $, including breakfast

THE MINIMALIST WHITE TRAVERTINE lobby of the Room Mate Alicia hotel, on Madrid's Plaza de Santa Ana, announces its overall aesthetic: high style on an intimate scale. A curlicue staircase rising through the space leads to 34 pastel-hued rooms accented with bold color. Blond-wood headboards contrast with the baby blue walls and coral throws. The two duplex suites have the same chic yet comfortable look, but with more space—terraces look out on the leafy square, and each comes with its own plunge pool.

A dining alcove in a suite at Madrid's Room Mate Alicia.

Above left: An interior courtyard at
Palacio Ca Sa Galesa. Above: The rooftop terrace.

PALACIO CA SA GALESA

Majorca, Spain

THE PALACIO CA SA GALESA HOTEL, IN THE MAJORCAN
town of Palma, is steeped in history. The 1576
building's 12 rooms and suites are furnished with
antiques, 17th-century artifacts are scattered
throughout the bar, and the spires of a centuries-
old cathedral loom above the rooftop terrace.
It's an ideal base from which to explore the city's
surrounding Gothic district—but it's also steps
from the Mediterranean, and no one could blame
you for choosing to just sunbathe instead.

*8 Carr. de Miramar, Palma, Majorca, Spain;
34/97-171-5400; palaciocasagalesa.com; doubles from $$*

A deluxe room in Athens's O&B Boutique Hotel. Right: A lobby view.

O&B BOUTIQUE HOTEL

Athens, Greece

7 Leokoriou St., Athens, Greece; 30-210/331-2950; oandbhotel.com; doubles from $$

SINCE THE 2004 OLYMPICS, ATHENS HAS UNDERGONE a face-lift, and the city is now hitting its stride with design-oriented restaurants, shops, and hotels. At the 11-room O&B Boutique Hotel, walking distance from the Parthenon, stream-lined dark brown furniture is juxtaposed with flashes of color: a scarlet curtain here, tangerine satin cushions there. That splashy exuberance matches the tenor of the vibe outside, in the up-and-coming Psyrri district. The lobby lounge and restaurant is a favorite meeting spot for area artists, who congregate over signature cocktails mixed from berries, vanilla, vodka, and juice.

MELENOS LINDOS

Rhodes, Greece

THE 12-ROOM WHITEWASHED Melenos Lindos is a quiet refuge in the popular town of Lindos, on the Grecian island of Rhodes. Designer Michalis Melenos drew from the area's mixed artistic heritage—Greek, Byzantine, Arabic, Ottoman— in creating the hotel. Ceilings are hand-stenciled, beds are carved by village craftsmen, and pathways are paved in beach-pebble mosaics. Melenos Lindos keeps a stash of antique walking sticks on hand for hikes to a nearby medieval fortress, but it is also set up for less demanding pursuits; a cliffside tented terrace has uninterrupted views of one of the island's most spectacular harbors.

Lindos, Rhodes, Greece; 30-22440/32222; melenoslindos.com; doubles from $$$

Melenos Lindos, overlooking the Aegean on the island of Rhodes.

DELTA NATURE RESORT

Danube Delta, Romania

Somova, Tulcea, Romania; 40-21/311-4532;
deltaresort.com; doubles from $$, including breakfast

THE DANUBE DELTA IS ONE OF THE CONTINENT'S LAST frontiers, an untamed tropical region with hundreds of wildlife species living among its wetlands, and just a handful of villages. Before the arrival of the Delta Nature Resort three years ago, there were practically no modern places to stay. The low-impact, 32-acre eco-lodge overlooks the apex of the Danube, about 180 miles northeast of Bucharest, and attracts a mix of nature lovers, sport fishermen, and wealthy Romanians. At a distance, the resort resembles a typical low-key fishing village, yet the 30 villas are outfitted with luxe but unobtrusive amenities and flourishes—jet-force showers, handmade carpets, polished wood furniture—that don't distract from the simple allure of having the setting, a vast expanse of nature, all to yourself.

The Angler's Bar at the Delta Nature Resort, in Romania. Opposite: The resort's main building.

GRAND HOTEL RODINA

Sochi, Russia

Above: The library of the Grand Hotel Rodina.
Left: An original 1950's chandelier in the lobby.

A LUXURIOUS REFURBISHMENT OF A STALIN-ERA villa, the 40-room Rodina is set on manicured grounds with a private beachfront in the year-round resort town of Sochi. Russian Hotels, an arm of billionaire aluminum oligarch Oleg Deripaska's empire, has imparted a postmodern patrician style: soaring ceilings, acres of creamy marble, exposed wood beams, and velvet- and leather-covered furniture. The hotel makes much of the local culture, with antique Cyrillic-language editions of Tolstoy and Pushkin in the library, and original iron doors painted with hammers and sickles in the lobby. Following the announcement that Sochi—between the Black Sea and Caucasus foothills—will be hosting the Winter Olympic Games in 2014, the hotel is sprucing up for its moment in the spotlight. Among the additions is a spa—complete with a traditional *banya,* or Russian bath—and an enormous indoor pool, part of the planned complex, is already open to guests.

33 Vinogradnaya St., Sochi, Russia; 7-8622/539-000; grandhotelrodina.ru; doubles from $$$, including breakfast

One of several pools at the Shangri-La Barr Al Jissah Resort & Spa, in Oman.

AFRICA+ THE MIDDLE EAST

An open-air tea
lounge at Adrère
Amellal Oasis.

ADRÈRE AMELLAL OASIS

Siwa, Egypt

A BEACON OF CONSERVATION, THIS SPARE Berber-style hotel on the Siwa Oasis was constructed as part of a local sustainable-development plan. An eight-hour drive west of Cairo, the fortress-like compound of 40 rooms is made of *kershef,* a heat-resistant mixture of rock salt and clay, and has stylish palm-beam roofs, beeswax candles, and stone floors covered in locally woven rugs. Since there is no electricity, pathways are lantern-lit at night, and braziers keep things warm. Underground Roman springs feed the pool. When the dunes of the bordering Great Sand Sea beckon, guides are available to lead Toyota Land Cruiser excursions; once in the middle of the undulating landscape, the driver will cut the engine and prepare a late-afternoon pot of mint tea, brewed with leaves grown organically on hotel grounds.

Siwa, Egypt; 20-2/2736-7879; adrereamellal.net; doubles from \$\$, including meals and activities

DAR EL MÉDINA

Tunis, Tunisia

TWO YEARS AGO, brothers Salah and Mustafa Belhaouane transformed their family mansion into the Dar El Médina, the first boutique hotel in Tunis's ancient quarter, a warren of cobblestoned streets, columned arches, and whitewashed houses. In the courtyard, well-dressed locals cluster at café tables to drink tea and puff from tall silver *shishas* (water pipes), which fill the air with aromatic smoke. The 12 quiet rooms and suites range in style from over-the-top Ottoman to Moorish minimalist and are as varied as the medina itself. One tiled staircase leads to a duplex with marble floors, Tunisian kilims, and hand-painted furniture; in the Douja suite, a crystal chandelier hangs from the ceiling, and archways are frosted with white-stucco arabesques.

64 Rue Sidi ben Arous, Tunis, Tunisia; 216-71/563-022; darelmedina.com; doubles from $, including breakfast

A guest
room at Dar
El Médina.

Dar Saïd's orange tree–shaded pool. Right: The reception area at Dar Dhiafa.

DAR SAÏD

Sidi Bou Saïd, Tunisia

THE 13TH-CENTURY HILL-TOWN RETREAT OF SIDI BOU Saïd, a few miles from Carthage, has stunning views of the Gulf of Tunis and razor-sharp light. The best way to experience the beauty of its exotic domes and sweetly scented gardens is to stay a night or two in one of Tunisia's most enchanting hotels. Located in a mid-19th-century mansion, Dar Saïd has been open since 1948, but was restored in 1998 with historically accurate materials like colorfully glazed faïence tiles and veined marble. The 24 rooms and suites look out onto patios dripping with vegetation and gurgling with fountains; all have simple antiques, Italian fabrics, and Tunisian carpets. The small swimming pool, in a garden shaded by orange trees, is a tranquil spot, especially in the height of the afternoon.

Rue Toumi, Sidi Bou Saïd, Tunisia; 216-71/729-666; darsaid.com.tn; doubles from $

DAR DHIAFA

Jerba, Tunisia

THE RESORT ISLAND OF JERBA, AN HOUR'S FLIGHT from Tunis, is known for its nine-mile beach lined with all-inclusive resorts whose guests rarely budge from the premises. Dar Dhiafa, however, is an exception. Located inland in the village of Erriadh and created from five adjoining houses, the hotel has unassuming interiors that are the last word in rustic chic—rough walls, asymmetrical rooms, funky Berber furniture—and grounds rampant with cacti growing in twisted curlicues. Most of the 15 rooms have wrought-iron platform beds and private patios facing one of two swimming pools; in suites, separate alcoves form a bedroom, salon, and dressing area. The sum total is a showpiece that surprises; there's another courtyard, tunnel, or lounge at every turn.

Erriadh, Jerba, Tunisia; 216-75/671-166; hoteldardhiafa.com; doubles from $

The Chief's House at Sanctuary at Ol Lentille, with West African feathered headdresses and Masai and Samburu tribal spears.

SANCTUARY AT OL LENTILLE

Laikipia Plateau, Kenya

THE KENYA OF ISAK DINESEN may be a thing of the past, but a private place in the country's lush hills can still be found. A 6,500-acre conservancy on the Laikipia Plateau is now home to four recherché rental villas and a spa. Each house is a kingdom unto itself, with its own pool and a dedicated staff that includes both a butler and a safari guide. Interiors are characterful and idiosyncratic: the Sultan's House has a papyrus-thatched roof, four-poster bed, and low-slung Moorish sofas, while the Colonel's House is furnished with campaign desks and English scroll armchairs. The property backs style with substance—the land-lease agreement preserves traditional Masai ways of life—and provides plenty of ways to explore the surroundings: game drives and guided tours on foot, horseback, and camelback. For less effort, you can peer through the GPS-controlled telescope on the viewing deck for a good look at Mount Kenya, 50 miles to the south.

Kijabe Group Ranch, Laikipia Plateau, Kenya; 888/588-4590; ol-lentille.com; houses from $$$$$

The pool and terrace at Clico Guest House.

CLICO GUEST HOUSE

Johannesburg, South Africa

THIS BOUTIQUE B&B in the leafy-chic Rosebank neighborhood is a refreshing departure from Johannesburg's other hotels in secure suburbs, which are typically flashy and pricey—and often soulless. Clico's handsome Cape Dutch façade has been preserved, but inside, owner Jeanette Schwegmann has added contemporary fizz. Antique Moroccan inlaid-wood tables flank sleek sofas and chairs by local designer Dilly Lills. The nine rooms all have balconies overlooking the jacaranda-filled grounds and are done in crisp ocher and beige tones; the gleaming white bathrooms are fitted with heating lights (useful in the surprisingly chilly highveld winters). Dine in the garden, where items from the French-inspired menu—such as lamb noisettes stuffed with herbs and garlic, smoked salmon on *Rösti* with crème fraîche, and hazelnut crème brûlée—are so popular that the restaurant has become a hot spot for area residents as well.

27 Sturdee Ave., Johannesburg, South Africa; 27-11/252-3300; clicoguesthouse.com; doubles from $, including breakfast

BARTHOLOMEUS KLIP FARMHOUSE

Hermon, South Africa

JUST OVER AN HOUR'S DRIVE northeast from Cape Town, this chic oasis in the up-and-coming Swartland wine region is the embodiment of rural respect-ability. The 17,000-acre farm and game reserve sits beside the Elandsberg mountains and abuts a lakelike reservoir that's ideal for fishing, windsurfing, and game drives. Family antiques fill the four-room Victorian homestead, a separate suite, and a stand-alone cottage, which are surrounded by wheat fields and fynbos heaths blooming with gladiolus and hyacinth. Inside, floral- and gingham-splashed fabrics accent rooms adjoining verandas wreathed in oak trees and rosebushes. The food in the dining room reflects a serious sense of place: Local wines are served with entrées made from ingredients sourced in the area, such as lemon beurre-blanc *kabeljou*, a native fish, or rack of Riebeek lamb from a nearby valley.

Bo-Hermon Rd., Hermon, Swartland, South Africa; 27-22/448-1820; bartholomeusklip.com; doubles from $$$, all-inclusive

The deck house overlooking the
Groenberg mountains, at Bartholomeus Klip.

The Studio at
Nina Café Suites.

NINA CAFÉ SUITES HOTEL

Tel Aviv, Israel

STOCKED WITH CUSTOM WOOD furnishings and bold, Art Deco–inspired textiles, the five suites at this stylish property fit right into the city's artsy Neve Tzedek neighborhood. Opened by the owners of boho-cool Nina Café across the street, it's one of the city's few boutique hotels, but it's got the laid-back feel of a pied-à-terre: there's no lobby (guests check in at reception through a separate entrance next door), and the uncluttered suites, reached via a red-carpeted staircase, start at an impressive 700 square feet. Slate-walled bathrooms, stone and white parquet floors, throw rugs from Afghanistan, and photographs and paintings by Israeli artists make for an unfussy, homegrown design mix. Step outside onto Shabazi Street, the area's winding main artery, and join locals trolling for cutting-edge fashion, jewelry, and housewares amid the red-tile-roofed buildings lining the lane.

29 Shabazi St., Tel Aviv, Israel; 972-52/508-4141; ninacafehotel.com; doubles from $$, including breakfast

SHANGRI-LA BARR AL JISSAH

Barr Al Jissah, Oman

OMAN IS IN MANY WAYS AN antique land. Even now, road maps are startlingly blank, a few highways intersected by faint lines that, in some cases, depict camel trails used for millennia. But the country's coast is fast becoming a regional destination, with lavish Dubai-style resorts that rise above the water's edge like mirages. On one stretch south of the capital, the Shangri-La hotel group has erected the Barr Al Jissah Resort & Spa in a setting that verges on magical. A man-made creek winds through the 124-acre grounds, a paradise of jasmine, date palms, and white umbrellas. Past the marble lobby lies a ribbon of talcum powder–white sand, bracketed by two rocky promontories. The complex consists of three hotel pods, each geared to a different type of guest (business, family, the ultra-elite), and a multinational staff will help set up a tennis match, organize a whale-watching excursion, or arrange for a rose petal–and-frankincense massage at the Chi spa.

Barr Al Jissah, Oman; 968/2477-6666; shangri-la.com; doubles from $$

Shangri-La
Barr Al Jissah's
reception area.

A breezeway leading to the Chedi Muscat's beach. Opposite: The hotel's reception desk.

CHEDI MUSCAT

Al Ghubra, Oman

TWENTY MILES NORTH OF THE OMANI CAPITAL of Muscat is a smooth, white, modern palace. Even at the end of the high season, when daytime temperatures start to creep above 100 degrees, the Chedi draws the region's wealthy, who come seeking an outpost of serenity and find hushed and airy corridors where Indonesian hardwood furniture mixes with dusky stone floors and minimalist vaulted arches. A holiday here gives the feeling of chic sequestration. Each of the 151 rooms has a commodious open-plan bathroom with a rain-forest shower and stunning views of either the biscuit-colored Hajar Mountains or the Gulf of Oman. At the private beach, or one of the two swimming pools, the white-

ASIA

Signature, the
French-influenced
restaurant
at the Mandarin
Oriental, Tokyo.

The tearoom at
the Mandarin
Oriental, Tokyo.

MANDARIN ORIENTAL, TOKYO

Tokyo, Japan

THERE'S A NEW CROP OF LUXURY HOTELS in Tokyo, and one of the most impressive is the Mandarin Oriental, in Nihonbashi—a business district in the northeastern part of the city. Occupying the top nine floors of a stunning tower designed by Cesar Pelli, the hotel has views that make the city look like one big Lego project. From 500 feet up, tiny toy cars whiz along video-game streets. Wherever you are—whether in one of the four restaurants, the high-tech fitness center, or the elaborate spa—oversize windows put the megalopolis in grand perspective. In the 179 rooms, neutral colors and ebonized wood furniture upholstered in beige chenille provide a soothing backdrop. The sophisticated design is inspired by nature: bedspreads are patterned with a fallen-leaf motif, and illumination from Echizen paper lampshades evokes moonlight.

2-1-1 Nihonbashi Muromachi, Chuo-ku, Tokyo, Japan; 800/526-6566 or 81-3/3270-8950; mandarinoriental.com; doubles from $$$

GRAND HYATT, TOKYO

Tokyo, Japan

THE **GRAND HYATT TOKYO** is right in the thick of things in Roppongi Hills, an urban development with more than 200 shops and restaurants and the contemporary Mori Art Museum. The neighboring bustle can be felt in the lobby, where bellmen in headsets serve as traffic conductors to a steady stream of stylish guests, including celebrities like Brad Pitt, Norah Jones, and Prince Albert. It's easy to see the attraction: the 389 rooms are quiet oases of earth tones, mahogany fixtures, and beige limestone baths. The mirrored, mazelike gym and spa is the work of Japanese architect Takashi Sugimoto, a.k.a. SuperPotato. And at the Maduro bar, the bartender crafts a perfect Manhattan, with real rye and a flawless round ice cube for slower melting.

Maduro, a bar at the Grand Hyatt, Tokyo, in Roppongi Hills.

6-10-3 Roppongi, Minato-ku, Tokyo, Japan; 800/233-1234 or 81-3/4333-1234; tokyo.grand.hyatt.com; doubles from $$$

A guest room at Peninsula Tokyo. Right: Hinokizaka, the Japanse restaurant at the Ritz-Carlton, Tokyo.

PENINSULA TOKYO

Tokyo, Japan

THE 314-ROOM PENINSULA, RIGHT ON THE IMPERIAL Palace Gardens, has a lock on location. The building, a granite-clad landmark, is rich in Japan's design heritage—from lattices on lobby walls to lacquered desks in the rooms. Equally impressive is the Peninsula's well-thought-out gadgetry, found throughout the hotel: cordless phones convert to mobiles for use off-site, coffee pod machines deliver round-the-clock espressos, and handy nail driers in the rooms enable expert manicures.

1-8-1 Yurakucho, Chiyoda-ku, Tokyo, Japan; 866/382-8388 or 81-3/6270-2288; peninsula.com; doubles from $$$

RITZ-CARLTON, TOKYO

Tokyo, Japan

PART OF TOKYO MIDTOWN, A $3 BILLION COMPLEX within walking distance of Roppongi Hills, the Ritz-Carlton, Tokyo occupies the city's tallest tower. Hyperbole continues inside; the 560-square-foot, beige-toned rooms are the city's largest, with five-star amenities—Frette sheets and featherbeds, rain showers, Bulgari toiletries, and Sony flat screens viewable from marble bathtubs. Though small, the lobby bar draws Japanese ladies dressed in head-to-toe labels, who wait patiently to take tea beneath 13-foot-tall paintings by Sam Francis.

9-7-1 Akasaka, Minato-ku, Tokyo, Japan; 800/241-3333 or 81-3/3423-8000; ritzcarlton.com; doubles from $$$

UTOCO DEEP SEA THERAPY CENTER & HOTEL

Muroto City, Japan

ON JAPAN'S SUBTROPICAL SHIKOKU ISLAND the late, famed makeup artist Shu Uemura created a 17-room spa and hotel dedicated to therapeutic treatments from the surrounding Pacific Ocean. The Modernist concrete-and-steel resort, designed by Paris- and Tokyo-based Ciel Rouge, arcs between the surf and a steep hillside, and views of the horizon are unobstructed. Water is pumped up from ocean depths and harnessed to fill pools and infuse algae and fango wraps with rich minerals. In the restaurant, big portholes look out at the shoreline as the staff serves smoked tofu dipped in Muroto salt, or grilled fish marinated in rice vinegar. At key points near reception and the spa, large open-air spaces allow offshore breezes and crashing waves to whisper, shell-like, in your ear.

6969-1 Murotomisaki-cho, Muroto City, Kochi, Japan; 81-8/8722-1811; utocods.co.jp; doubles from $$, including breakfast

Utoco, a spa hotel
on Shikoku Island.

OYADO KINENKAN

Nagano, Japan

An Oyado
Kinenkan guest
room set
up for dinner.

JAPAN'S TRADITIONAL COUNTRY INNS, *ryokan*, are intimate establishments that typically include elaborate breakfast and dinner service. While many have recently been updated to remain relevant in the modern age, the centuries-old Oyado Kinenkan, on a quiet backstreet of Nagano, in the foothills of the Japanese Alps, is staying true to its roots. Its ancient wood floors and ceiling beams are evocative of a Japan that is rapidly disappearing. Rooms with large windows and unembellished, low-lying furnishings make the most of the peaceful surroundings. Though the setting is spare, the service is elaborate. Harue Watanabe, the charming *okami,* or inn mistress, is likely to appear at any moment with a plate of sweet bean pastry, and wait for you to sample and signal your approval with a smile.

550 Nishi-machi, Nagano, Japan;
81-26/234-2043; from $ per person

YOSHI-IMA

Kyoto, Japan

Tea ceremony at
the Yoshi-ima *ryokan*.
Opposite: The
entrance to the inn.

WHILE IT HAS TINKERED WITH tradition in order to compete with an influx of international hotels, Yoshi-ima, a 19th-century *ryokan* in Kyoto's Gion district, still feels like something out of another era. A group of kimono-clad women will lead you to your spacious room, in all its minimalist beauty—paper blinds; low, cushion-covered stools; a futon. The elaborate *kaiseki* dinner, included in the price of your stay, arrives slowly, some of it in shiny lacquer boxes, and is composed of seasonal delicacies: mountain potatoes, bundles of mushrooms, and grilled gingko nuts. While you sip sake, you can look out onto a jewel of a garden filled with shimmering bamboo trees.

Shinmonzen, Gion, Kyoto, Japan; 81-75/561-2620; yoshi-ima.co.jp; $ per person, including meals

MANDARIN ORIENTAL, HONG KONG

Hong Kong, China

Right: A member of
the staff at the Mandarin
Oriental, Hong Kong.
Below: A renovated guest
room. Opposite: Man
Wah restaurant, on the
hotel's top floor.

world's best

FEW HOTELS HAVE DEFINED A CITY
as much as the Mandarin Oriental
has Hong Kong. Since opening
in 1963, its lobby has been populated at all
hours by a glittering cast of casino mag-
nates, tea-sipping socialites, Continental
royalty, and visiting celebrities. But by
the new millennium the hotel's infrastruc-
ture had become outmoded and in need
of updating. The Singapore firm of Lim, Teo
& Wilkes (responsible for the face-lift of
the Taj Mahal Palace & Tower in Mumbai)
was enlisted to perform a $140 million
renovation. The lobby still retains its Venini
chandeliers and gilded panels depicting
Chinese folk scenes—but a closer look
reveals bolder colors and richer textures:
mink-hued upholstery, polished walnut,
glowing orange lacquer. The Mandarin Grill
has been reworked by Terence Conran.
Balconies have been enclosed to provide
more indoor space in some of the 502 guest
rooms, and the bathrooms are larger and `
more opulent. Wood-paneled living areas
are furnished with leather armchairs
and outsize Chinese desks. It's a whole new
Mandarin that's fresh, sexy, and perfect
for today's Hong Kong.

*5 Connaught Rd., Central, Hong Kong; 866/526-6567
or 852/2522-0111; mandarinoriental.com;
doubles from $$*

A villa with a
private plunge pool
at the Nam Hai.

NAM HAI

Hoi An, Vietnam

A HIGH-DESIGN PROPERTY HAS ARRIVED ON THE SOUTH CHINA SEA, and its sleek style is a testament to the impressive talent behind its inception. Aman resorts founder Adrian Zecha, French architect Reda Amalou, and Indonesian interior designer Jaya Ibrahim (whose past projects include the Chedi Milan) all collaborated on the Nam Hai's 100 freestanding villas, which are made from local woods, with elaborate hand-carved screens, pressed-eggshell surfaces, and stone floors. The property sits on a remote beach in Central Vietnam outside the quaint town of Hoi An—once a 16th-century trading port—and houses three swimming pools and a spa with sublime overwater relaxation rooms. Cool extras include luscious wool-and-cotton-blend bathrobes and outdoor showers. Executive chef Christine Townsend's eclectic dishes run the gamut from Vietnamese-style snapper carpaccio to Indian curry—helping to make this one of the most exciting newcomers around.

Hoi An, Quang Nam, Vietnam; 84-510/940-000; ghmhotels.com; doubles from $$$$

LA VERANDA GRAND MERCURE RESORT & SPA

Phu Quoc, Vietnam

FROM THE AIR, PHU QUOC, AN ISLAND IN THE GULF of Thailand, registers as a bright-green paint drop, ringed by flecks of ivory and splashed on a turquoise canvas. It's a quiet, humble spot that recently welcomed a well-heeled new resident: the $4.2 million, 43-room La Veranda Grand Mercure Resort & Spa. The look is cheery French colonial: yellow walls, terra-cotta tiles, and paddle fans stirring the air. The better guest rooms are set in single-story villas on a gently graded hillside above the beach, with ocean views, 14-foot cathedral ceilings, teak canopy beds, and big bathrooms. The fragrance of jasmine and frangipani wafts around the 2½-acre grounds, where heliconia, bougainvillea, and birds-of-paradise shade the brick paths. In contrast to the rough, dusty road beyond the hotel, the setting is pure tropical bliss.

Tran Hung Dao St., Duong Dong Beach, Phu Quoc, Vietnam; 800/221-4542 or 84-77/398-2988; laverandaresort.com; doubles from $$

A canopy bed
in a guest room
at La Veranda.
Opposite: The
property's beach.

The lobby
at Luxx.

LUXX

Bangkok, Thailand

THIS MODERN-ORIENTAL-STYLE GUESTHOUSE, in a former office building near Silom
Road, is entered through heavy wood doors that lead to a glossy bi-level reception
hall. In the lobby, guests sprawl on angular couches, paging through Australian
fashion mags and surfing the Web on Wi-Fi–connected laptops. Most of the 13 silver-
and slate–accented rooms are set up like studio apartments: a partition separates
the teak soaking tubs and waterfall showers from the living space; the small writing
table next to the minibar doubles as a vanity. The room to book: No. 12, a junior suite
with windows that overlook a rock garden, and a sound system that's iPod-ready.

6/11 Decho Rd., Bangruk, Bangkok, Thailand; 66-2/635-8800; staywithluxx.com; doubles from $

A room at the Arun Residence. Left: The game lodge–inspired lobby of the Eugenia.

THE EUGENIA

Bangkok, Thailand

IF YOU FUSED THE GRANDEUR OF COLONIAL INDIA WITH the simplicity of an African game lodge, the results would look much like the Eugenia. Animal trophies cover the walls, brass light fixtures are imported from the Subcontinent, and an old-fashioned metal shower sits next to the sleek pool in the hotel's lush backyard. The eclectic mix continues in the 12 rooms, most of which are done up with four-poster beds, antique wooden desks, and framed vintage maps. Forgo rickety tuk-tuks in exchange for a chauffeured spin in one of the hotel's vintage cars: the fleet includes a 1970 Daimler limousine, a 1958 Mercedes Ponton, and a 1965 S-Type Jaguar.

267 Soi Sukhumvit 31, North Klongtan, Wattana, Bangkok, Thailand; 66-2/259-9011; theeugenia.com; doubles from $

ARUN RESIDENCE

Bangkok, Thailand

HIDDEN ON A SMALL RESIDENTIAL STREET IN THE Old City, this quaint four-story hotel abuts the Chao Phraya River and has an open lobby with views of Wat Arun, the 19th-century Temple of the Dawn. The four guest rooms combine Asian and European design styles to relaxed yet elegant effect: futon beds and French doors, dark wood floors and white-paneled walls, botanical prints and traditional Thai cushions. In the only suite, yards of diaphanous curtains frame a wide private terrace lined with pots of palms. Wake up early for a picture-perfect sunrise over the spires of Wat Arun.

36–38 Soi Pratoo Nok Yoong, Maharat Rd., Rattanakosin Island, Bangkok, Thailand; 66-2/221-9158; arunresidence.com; doubles from $

FOUR SEASONS RESORT KOH SAMUI

Koh Samui, Thailand

THE FOUR SEASONS'S FIRST THAI BEACH RESORT marks a turning point for Koh Samui. Secluded on the island's northwest corner, the hotel is sheltered from the clamor of nearby beaches. Landscape designer–turned-architect Bill Bensley, who also created the Four Seasons Tented Camp in Chiang Rai, is responsible for both the resort's elegant look and the sublime water views from all public spaces. The 60 villas are propped on stilts, with infinity pools, teak floors, and rosewood furniture; they're the most expensive on the island, but worth it for the views alone.

219 Moo 5, Tumbon Anthong, Thailand; 800/332-3442 or 66-77/243-000; fourseasons.com; doubles from $$$

A villa at Four Seasons Resort Koh Samui.

A suite at Indigo Pearl, on Phuket.

INDIGO PEARL

Phuket, Thailand

Nai Yang Beach, Phuket, Thailand; 66-76/327-006; indigo-pearl.com; doubles from $

INDIGO PEARL'S ROUGH-HEWN AESTHETIC WAS inspired by its past: architect Bill Bensley (who also worked on the Four Seasons Koh Samui, left) played upon the site's history as a tin mine when he retrofitted the 277-room property with polished-concrete floors, steel beams, and machinery-inspired sculptures. The industrial austerity is tempered by glimmering Thai silks on pillows and chairs, plush beds, and freestanding bathtubs. The complex includes a cooking school, fitness center, library, full-service spa, and a kid's club, providing a whole slew of leisurely pursuits.

MAHUA KOTHI

Madhya Pradesh, India

THE OPENING OF THE LUXURY LODGE MAHUA Kothi came not a moment too soon for seasoned travelers who've done all the African safari lodges. Africa has its Big Five—but only India delivers the tiger. Just outside the national park of Bandhavgarh (Kipling country and the setting for *The Jungle Book*), the lodge is a joint venture between Taj Hotels Resorts and Palaces, the Nepalese industrialist Binod Chaudhary, and Conservation Corporation Africa. The 12 cottages—on 40 bamboo-covered acres—are modeled after *kutiyas*, traditional jungle dwellings. Inside, wooden puppets from Kerala hang on the walls, niches are filled with collections of amber-glass doorknobs, and a massive *sal* tree trunk sliced in half lengthwise doubles as a vanity in the bathroom. The staff manages the nearly impossible task of delivering service that's human, subtle, and comprehensive all at the same time. Guests rarely dine in the same place twice: tables are set up on the roof of the main pavilion; beside the beautiful crumbling brick wall of the kitchen garden; or in a field under an ancient mahua tree.

Tala, Madhya Pradesh, India; 866/969-1825; ccafrica.com; $$$$ per person, including meals

Mahua Kothi's terrace. Opposite, above: A cottage bedroom. Opposite, below: A rooftop lounge.

W RETREAT & SPA MALDIVES

Fesdu Island, Maldives

THE DESIGN-SAVVY W HOTELS GROUP HAS EXPANDED TO THE South Seas with a private-island resort in the Maldives. The traditional structures were built with modern materials—tented Teflon fiber ceilings that resemble soaring white sails at the Away Spa replace thatch and wood. Each of the 78 overwater and beach villas comes with its own infinity or plunge pool, and they all have curving decks that take in stunning beach and ocean views. Moroccan poufs with red piping and saturated abstract paintings punctuate white linen and simple wicker furniture. Straightforward and youthful, it's taking W in a new direction.

Fesdu Island, Maldives; 877/946-8357 or 011-960/666-2222; whotels. com; doubles from $$$$$

A deck and
outdoor seating
area at the
W Retreat & Spa
Maldives.

AUSTRALIA+
NEW ZEALAND

Whare Kea Lodge,
overlooking Lake Wanaka on
New Zealand's South Island.

QUALIA

Hamilton Island, Australia

A deck with views of the Coral Sea, at Qualia. Left: A bungalow bedroom.

BORDERING THE GREAT BARRIER REEF, HAMILTON Island has long been a popular vacation spot. And now Qualia, a 60-bungalow retreat on the secluded northern shore, is helping redefine Aussie luxury. Owner Robert Oatley, founder of Rosemount Estate wines, invested about $65 million, hiring some of Australia's leading designers to create a richly spare hotel where *kwila* hardwood, granite, and hoop pine emphasize the surrounding landscape. Qualia's name comes from the Latin word meaning "a collection of sensory experiences"; the prevailing ethos here is one of deep, restorative calm. Expansive windows maximize Coral Sea views, and the sound of lapping waves can be heard from open-air breezeways, patios, and terraces.

Hamilton Island, Australia; 61-2/9433-3349; qualiaresort.com; doubles from $$$$$, including meals

The exterior of Craig's Royal Hotel in Ballarat, near Melbourne. Right: Lilianfels Blue Mountains.

CRAIG'S ROYAL HOTEL

Ballarat, Australia

SINCE 1853, CRAIG'S ROYAL HOTEL HAS ANCHORED historic Lydiard Street in the town of Ballarat, about an hour northwest of Melbourne. The property's recent four-year, $3 million renovation erased years' worth of out-of-character add-ons, introducing a grandeur to the interiors that matches the elegant façade. In the 41 rooms, dropped ceilings were stripped back, revealing sweeping arches. Elsewhere, restored brickwork and uncovered marble fireplaces recall the high-flying times of Australia's Gold Rush era, when the hotel first opened, and have brought the property back to its original Victorian glory.

10 Lydiard St. S., Ballarat, Australia; 61-3/5331-1377; craigsroyal.com.au; doubles from $

LILIANFELS BLUE MOUNTAINS

Katoomba, Australia

POSITIONED ON A BLUFF IN SOUTHEAST Australia's Blue Mountains National Park, Lilianfels is a country house built in 1889 that has been converted into an 85-room resort and spa, set on two acres of English-style gardens. The proper British aesthetic continues inside: guest rooms, many with gorgeous views of the Jamison Valley, are filled with overstuffed furniture and antique floral prints. In the cream-toned lounge, you can hang out by the fireplace and take in an equally panoramic view while enjoying a steaming cup of jasmine tea, fresh scones, and homemade jam.

Lilianfels Ave., Katoomba, Australia; 800/237-1236 or 61-2/4780-1200; lilianfels.com.au; doubles from $$$

The lobby at the Moondance Lodge. Right: A Rawnsley Park guest room.

MOONDANCE LODGE

Yallingup, Australia

MOONDANCE LODGE IS AN OUTPOST OF CIVILIZED style in the southwestern Margaret River wine region, a gum tree–flecked area where vintners bottle superior Shiraz. The main structure, on 33 acres, is built using indigenous materials: bathroom tiles are made from local ceramic, and Jarrah wood posts are used throughout. Most of the nine suites have private decks surrounded by native bush. There's also a gently graded on-site orchard, fragrant with lavender, where guests are encouraged to pluck peaches and plums right off the trees.

Spencer Rd., Yallingup, Australia; 61-8/9750-1777; moondancelodge.com; doubles from $$, including breakfast

RAWNSLEY PARK STATION

Flinders Ranges National Park, Australia

JUST A FEW HOURS NORTH OF ADELAIDE, THE FLINDERS Ranges National Park is known for high peaks, cavernous ravines, and wildlife-dotted plains. Two years ago, Tony and Julieanne Smith turned part of Rawnsley Park Station, their 7,500-acre sheep-shearing outpost adjoining the park, into a stunning eco-retreat. Four villas, constructed with recycled timber and straw-bale insulation, have retractable canvas ceilings that open up to reveal starry skies. Two of the park's biggest thrills are minutes away: Wilpena Pound, a 20,000-acre quartzite amphitheater, and the 500-foot sandstone face of Moonarie cliff, a rock climber's dream.

Wilpena Rd., Wilpena Pound, Australia; 61-8/8648-0030; rawnsleypark.com.au; doubles from $$, including breakfast

A balcony looking onto the Chamberlain Gorge, at El Questro Homestead.

EL QUESTRO HOMESTEAD

East Kimberley, Australia

REFINED COMFORT HAS ARRIVED IN THE outback. El Questro Homestead is a soothing six-room refuge in million-acre El Questro Wilderness Park, set amid vast manicured lawns and leafy gardens. The hotel's timber verandas, linen-covered furniture, and recycled wood beds bring a rustic yet contemporary feel to the bush. There are plenty of opportunities for getting up close and personal with nature, including hikes to Champagne Springs and soaks in the thermal pools of Zebedee Springs, which local Aborigines believe have healing qualities. You could also absorb it all in one fell swoop: scenic helicopter flights are the only way to access some distant water holes, making for a lofty immersion into the park's vast and varied terrain.

East Kimberley, Australia; 61-2/8296-8010; elquestrohomestead.com; doubles from $$$$$, including meals and some activities

TAKATU LODGE & VINEYARD

Matakana, New Zealand

The dining room in the main house at Takatu Lodge. Opposite: A guest-room bed.

ABOUT AN HOUR'S DRIVE NORTH OF AUCKLAND, Matakana is fast becoming a favorite wine destination. Heather and John Forsman visited 23 inns across New Zealand and Australia before opening Takatu Lodge. A Maori word meaning "well-prepared," Takatu has only four rooms, and you can't go wrong with any of them; each makes the most of the lodge's location, on a gorgeous vineyard. Bathtubs look out on the vines, and public spaces are uncluttered and serene. In the glass-walled sitting and dining room, guests gather for three-course breakfasts that can include homemade muesli or ricotta pancakes with fruit. And just outside, a poured-concrete patio has furniture arranged around a huge hearth—perfect for an evening tasting of the estate's Pinot Gris.

518 Whitmore Rd., Matakana, New Zealand; 64-9/423-0299; takatulodge.co.nz; doubles from $$, including breakfast and wine tasting

HUKA LODGE

Taupo, New Zealand

The living room
of the four-bedroom
Owner's Cottage, at
Huka Lodge. Right:
The cottage entryway.

IF ROYAL FAVOR COUNTS AS A BAROMETER of a hotel's success, then Huka Lodge is a clear winner: Queen Elizabeth II has stayed here five times, and former U.S. presidents also pepper its confidential guest list. The appeal is clear: the hotel, near Lake Taupo on the North Island, along the Waikato River, is renowned for its Scottish Highlands–style setting and rich trout fishing. Each of the 20 rooms is done in a creamy white palette, with down duvet–covered beds, dressing rooms, and slatted wooden terraces that open onto a lawn flowing down to the river's edge. At night, with the door ajar, the sound of the rushing Waikato lulls pampered guests into a deep sleep.

Huka Falls Road, Taupo, New Zealand; 800/525-4800 or 64-7/378-5791; hukalodge.com; doubles from $$$$$, including breakfast and dinner

WHARE KEA LODGE

Wanaka, New Zealand

The Chalet at Whare Kea
Lodge, atop the Buchanan
mountain range.

THE WORD SPECTACULAR SEEMS INADEQUATE TO describe Wanaka and the neighboring Southern Lakes District on New Zealand's South Island. Originally built as a holiday home for members of the Myer family, Melbourne's original retail dynasty, Whare Kea is New Zealand luxury at its understated best. An in-house chef provides guests with breakfast and dinner daily, and each of the six suites has a view over manicured grounds that drop away to the shores of Lake Wanaka. For even more dramatic vistas, guests can spend a night in the hotel's alpine chalet, isolated at 5,600 feet and accessible only by helicopter and cross-country skis.

Mount Aspiring Rd., Wanaka, New Zealand; 800/735-2478 or 64-3/443-1400; wharekealodge.com; doubles from $$$$$

The Hotel Santa Caterina's pool, on the Bay of Amalfi, in Italy.

WORLD'S BEST

IN *TRAVEL + LEISURE*'S ANNUAL WORLD'S BEST AWARDS SURVEY, READERS ARE ASKED TO RATE THEIR FAVORITE HOTELS AND SPAS AROUND THE WORLD, BASED ON LOCATION, FOOD, WINE, SERVICE, AND VALUE, AMONG OTHER CRITERIA. EACH YEAR, THE CHANGING LIST OF WINNERS REVEALS READERS' EVOLVING, BUT ALWAYS EXACTING, STANDARDS OF EXCELLENCE. YOU'LL FIND THE MOST RECENT RESULTS ON THE FOLLOWING PAGES, ORGANIZED BY REGION AND RANKED ON A SCALE OF 0 TO 100.

THE RANKINGS

The lobby terrace at the Oriental, in Bangkok.

TOP 100 HOTELS

The entrance
courtyard of the
Oberoi Udaivilas,
in Udaipur, India.

1 **OBEROI UDAIVILAS** Udaipur, India **94.36**
2 **SINGITA SABI SAND/KRUGER NATIONAL PARK***
South Africa **94.30**
3 **THE ORIENTAL** Bangkok **94.23**
4 **FOUR SEASONS HOTEL ISTANBUL AT SULTANAHMET 93.55**
5 **MILESTONE HOTEL** London **93.06** ★
6 **IL FALCONIERE** Cortona, Italy **92.97**
7 **SABI SABI PRIVATE GAME RESERVE** Sabi Sands,
South Africa **92.81**
8 **MANDARIN ORIENTAL** Munich **92.73** ★
9 **FOUR SEASONS RESORT HUALALAI** Hawaii **92.65**
10 **OBEROI AMARVILAS** Agra, India **92.56**
11 **OBEROI RAJVILAS** Jaipur, India **92.50**
12 **PENINSULA BANGKOK 92.41**
13 **CHÂTEAU LES CRAYÈRES** Reims, France **92.39**
14 **JUMBY BAY, A ROSEWOOD RESORT** Antigua **92.24**
15 **FOUR SEASONS HOTEL GRESHAM PALACE** Budapest **92.15**
16 **MOMBO CAMP** Moremi Game Reserve, Botswana **92.08**
17 **TU TU' TUN LODGE** Gold Beach, Oregon **92.05**
18 **FOUR SEASONS HOTEL CAIRO AT NILE PLAZA 92.00**
19 **FOUR SEASONS RESORT** Chiang Mai, Thailand **91.90**
20 **CAPE GRACE** Cape Town **91.52**
21 **MALAMALA GAME RESERVE** Mpumalanga, South Africa **91.38**
22 **LADERA** St. Lucia **91.34**
23 **LA CASA QUE CANTA** Zihuatanejo, Mexico **91.28**
24 **KICHWA TEMBO** Masai Mara, Kenya **91.25**
25 **LE SIRENUSE** Positano, Italy **91.18**
26 **NGORONGORO CRATER LODGE** Tanzania **91.11**
27 **WOODLANDS RESORT & INN** Summerville,
South Carolina **91.09**
28 **FOUR SEASONS HOTEL** Prague **91.07**
29 **FOUR SEASONS HOTEL GEORGE V** Paris **91.05**
30 **FOUR SEASONS HOTEL** Amman, Jordan **90.95**
31 **41** London **90.68** ★
32 **POST HOTEL & SPA** Lake Louise, Alberta **90.61**
33 **RITZ-CARLTON MILLENIA** Singapore **90.59**
34 **THE STRAND** Yangon, Myanmar **90.56** ★
35 **SWEETWATERS TENTED CAMP** Sweetwaters Game Reserve,
Kenya **90.50**
36 **BLANTYRE** Lenox, Massachusetts **90.43**
37 **PENINSULA HONG KONG 90.37**
38 **HALEKULANI** Honolulu, Oahu **90.29**
39 **LONDOLOZI PRIVATE GAME RESERVE** Sabi Sands,
South Africa **90.19**
40 **RAFFLES HOTEL** Singapore **90.15**
41 **FOUR SEASONS HOTEL CAIRO AT THE FIRST RESIDENCE 90.14**
42 **FOUR SEASONS HOTEL** Buenos Aires **90.12**
43 **SANCTUARY AT KIAWAH ISLAND GOLF RESORT**
South Carolina **90.07**
44 **TORTILIS CAMP** Amboseli National Park, Kenya **90.00** ★
45 **PENINSULA BEVERLY HILLS 89.99**
46 **FOUR SEASONS HOTEL** Bangkok **89.93**
47 **KIRAWIRA LUXURY TENTED CAMP** Serengeti National Park,
Tanzania **89.92**
48 **FAIRMONT MARA SAFARI CLUB** Masai Mara, Kenya **89.87**

CONTINUED FROM PAGE 197

49 JAMAICA INN Ocho Rios, Jamaica **89.78**
50 FOUR SEASONS RESORT MAUI AT WAILEA **89.72**
51 ESPERANZA Los Cabos, Mexico **89.68**
52 IL PELLICANO Porto Ercole, Italy **89.64**★
53 PLANTERS INN Charleston, South Carolina **89.64**†
54 INN AT SPANISH BAY Pebble Beach, California **89.63**
55 FOUR SEASONS RESORT Jackson Hole, Wyoming **89.50**
56 JAO CAMP Moremi Game Reserve, Botswana **89.47** ★
57 HÔTEL D'EUROPE Avignon, France **89.42**
58 HUKA LODGE Taupo, New Zealand **89.38**
59 CHÂTEAU DE LA CHÈVRE D'OR Èze Village, France **89.35**
60 FOUR SEASONS RESORT LANAI, THE LODGE AT KOELE **89.29**
61 TABLE BAY HOTEL Cape Town **89.23**
62 HÔTEL HERMITAGE Monte Carlo **89.14**
63 MADRONA MANOR Healdsburg, California **89.09**
64 LA BASTIDE DE MOUSTIERS Moustiers-Ste.-Marie,
   France **89.04**
65 DOMAINE DES HAUTS DE LOIRE Onzain, France **89.00**
65 LE QUARTIER FRANÇAIS Franschhoek, South Africa **89.00** ★
67 HÔTEL DU CAP EDEN-ROC Antibes, France **88.89**
68 RITZ-CARLTON Santiago, Chile **88.86**
69 MALLIOUHANA HOTEL & SPA Anguilla **88.86**
70 FOUR SEASONS RESORT LANAI AT MANELE BAY** **88.86**
71 FOUR SEASONS RESORT BALI AT JIMBARAN BAY **88.83**
72 IL SAN PIETRO Positano, Italy **88.82**
73 HOTEL SAINT-BARTH ISLE DE FRANCE St. Bart's **88.81**
74 EDEN ROCK HOTEL St. Bart's **88.70**
75 THE WESTCLIFF Johannesburg **88.68**
76 BLACKBERRY FARM Walland, Tennessee **88.62**
77 FULLERTON HOTEL Singapore **88.61**
78 RITZ-CARLTON Istanbul **88.60** ★
79 SHANGRI-LA'S FAR EASTERN PLAZA HOTEL Taipei **88.59**
80 WILLOWS LODGE Woodinville, Washington **88.57**★
80 BEAU-RIVAGE PALACE Lausanne, Switzerland **88.57**
82 TAJ LAKE PALACE Udaipur, India **88.55**
83 HORNED DORSET PRIMAVERA Rincón, Puerto Rico **88.54**
84 AUBERGE SAINT-ANTOINE Quebec City **88.52**★
85 FOUR SEASONS HOTEL Hong Kong **88.50**
86 PENINSULA CHICAGO **88.38**
87 BERNARDUS LODGE Carmel Valley, California **88.37**
88 ONE & ONLY PALMILLA Los Cabos, Mexico **88.32**
89 SHANGRI-LA HOTEL Bangkok **88.28**
90 HOTEL VILLA CIPRIANI Asolo, Italy **88.27**
91 FOUR SEASONS HOTEL Singapore **88.24**
92 HOTEL HASSLER Rome **88.18**
93 GLENEAGLES HOTEL Auchterarder, Scotland **88.18**
94 KATIKIES HOTEL Santorini, Greece **88.17**★
95 RITZ-CARLTON Berlin **88.17**★
96 FOUR SEASONS RESORT Nevis **88.10**
97 FOUR SEASONS HOTEL Shanghai **88.08**
98 FOUR SEASONS HOTEL Chicago **88.03**
99 MOUNT NELSON HOTEL Cape Town **87.94**
100 GRAVETYE MANOR HOTEL West Sussex, England **87.92**

The pool deck overlooking the Caribbean at Ladera, on St. Lucia.

* Formerly Singita Private Game Reserve, South Africa.
**Formerly Manele Bay Hotel, Lanai.
†Throughout the World's Best Awards, scores are rounded
to the nearest hundredth of a point; in the event of an exact tie,
properties, companies, or destinations share the same ranking.
★ Denotes a debut in the World's Best Awards.

An outdoor fireplace at Mii Amo, in Sedona, Arizona.

TOP 15 DESTINATION SPAS

1. **MII AMO, A DESTINATION SPA AT ENCHANTMENT RESORT** Sedona, Arizona **86.86**
2. **LES SOURCES DE CAUDALIE** Bordeaux-Martillac, France **85.59**
3. **ALDER THERMAE SPA RESORT** Siena, Italy **85.59**
4. **MIRAVAL RÉSORT** Tucson, Arizona **85.26**
5. **CANYON RANCH** Tucson, Arizona **84.80**
6. **CHIVA-SOM INTERNATIONAL HEALTH RESORT** Hua Hin, Thailand **84.75**
7. **PLATEAU AT GRAND HYATT** Hong Kong **83.24**
8. **GREEN VALLEY SPA & RESORT** St. George, Utah **83.00**
9. **LAKE AUSTIN SPA RESORT** Austin, Texas **82.67**
10. **RANCHO LA PUERTA** Tecate, Mexico **82.25**
11. **CANYON RANCH** Lenox, Massachusetts **82.23**
12. **MAYFLOWER INN & SPA** Washington, Connecticut **82.02**
13. **LODGE AT WOODLOCH** Hawley, Pennsylvania **80.75**
14. **MAYA TULUM** Tulum, Mexico **79.49**
15. **GOLDEN DOOR** Escondido, California **78.59**

UNITED STATES+ CANADA

TOP 100 HOTELS

Stairway leading
to the lobby of
the Greenbrier,
in West Virginia.

1 **TU TU' TUN LODGE** Gold Beach, Oregon **92.05**

2 **WOODLANDS RESORT & INN** Summerville,
South Carolina **91.09**

3 **POST HOTEL & SPA** Lake Louise, Alberta **90.61**

4 **BLANTYRE** Lenox, Massachusetts **90.43**

5 **SANCTUARY AT KIAWAH ISLAND GOLF RESORT**
South Carolina **90.07**

6 **PENINSULA BEVERLY HILLS 89.99**

7 **PLANTERS INN** Charleston, South Carolina **89.64**

8 **INN AT SPANISH BAY** Pebble Beach, California **89.63**

9 **FOUR SEASONS RESORT** Jackson Hole, Wyoming **89.50**

10 **MADRONA MANOR** Healdsburg, California **89.09**

11 **BLACKBERRY FARM** Walland, Tennessee **88.62**

12 **WILLOWS LODGE** Woodinville, Washington **88.57** ★

13 **AUBERGE SAINT-ANTOINE** Quebec City **88.52** ★

14 **PENINSULA CHICAGO 88.38**

15 **BERNARDUS LODGE** Carmel Valley, California **88.37**

16 **FOUR SEASONS HOTEL** Chicago **88.03**

17 **AUBERGE DU SOLEIL** Rutherford, California **87.91**

18 **INN AT LITTLE WASHINGTON** Washington, Virginia **87.83**

19 **COLUMBIA GORGE HOTEL** Hood River, Oregon **87.76** ★

20 **MARQUESA HOTEL** Key West, Florida **87.70**

21 **WICKANINNISH INN** Tofino, Vancouver Island **87.64**

22 **ST. REGIS HOTEL** New York City **87.59**

23 **THE LOWELL** New York City **87.41**

24 **FOUR SEASONS RESORT** Whistler, British Columbia **87.40**

25 **THE CLOISTER AT SEA ISLAND** Georgia **87.26**

26 **STEIN ERIKSEN LODGE** Park City, Utah **87.18**

27 **CAMPTON PLACE HOTEL** San Francisco **87.00**

28 **LITTLE NELL** Aspen, Colorado **86.99**

29 **LITTLE PALM ISLAND RESORT & SPA** Little Torch Key,
Florida **86.81**

30 **ST. REGIS RESORT** Aspen, Colorado **86.78**

31 **SALISH LODGE & SPA** Snoqualmie, Washington **86.55**

32 **SOOKE HARBOUR HOUSE** Sooke, Vancouver Island **86.39**

33 **INN ON BILTMORE ESTATE** Asheville, North Carolina **86.38**

34 **INN AT PALMETTO BLUFF** Bluffton, South Carolina **86.33** ★

35 **BELLAGIO** Las Vegas **86.31**

36 **FOUR SEASONS RESORT SCOTTSDALE AT TROON NORTH**
Arizona **86.30**

37 **SAN YSIDRO RANCH, A ROSEWOOD RESORT**
Santa Barbara, California **86.30**

38 **RITZ-CARLTON, LAGUNA NIGUEL** Dana Point,
California **86.22**

39 **RITZ-CARLTON, BATTERY PARK** New York City **86.17**

40 **WENTWORTH MANSION** Charleston, South Carolina **86.17**

41 **GREYFIELD INN** Cumberland Island, Georgia **86.11** ★

42 **RUSTY PARROT LODGE & SPA** Jackson Hole, Wyoming **86.03**

43 **INN AT MONTCHANIN VILLAGE** Montchanin, Delaware **86.00**

44 **WATERCOLOR INN** Santa Rosa Beach, Florida **85.97**

45 **FOUR SEASONS HOTEL** New York City **85.89**

46 **FOUR SEASONS HOTEL** Las Vegas **85.86**

47 **RITZ-CARLTON** Chicago (A Four Seasons Hotel) **85.85**

48 **FOUR SEASONS HOTEL** Austin **85.79**

49 **FOUR SEASONS HOTEL** Boston **85.75**

50 **RITZ-CARLTON LODGE, REYNOLDS PLANTATION**
Greensboro, Georgia **85.74**

51 **POST RANCH INN** Big Sur, California **85.73**

52 **THE BROADMOOR** Colorado Springs **85.68**

53 **RITZ-CARLTON** San Francisco **85.67**

54 **LODGE & CLUB AT PONTE VEDRA BEACH** Florida **85.66**

55 **FEARRINGTON HOUSE COUNTRY INN**
Pittsboro, North Carolina **85.65**

56 **FOUR SEASONS HOTEL** San Francisco **85.43**

57 **RICHMOND HILL INN** Asheville, North Carolina **85.42**

58 **VENTANA INN & SPA** Big Sur, California **85.35**

59 **XV BEACON** Boston **85.33**

60 **MANDARIN ORIENTAL** Miami **85.33**

61 **THE GREENBRIER** White Sulphur Springs, West Virginia **85.32**

62 **RITZ-CARLTON** Naples, Florida **85.29**

63 **TRUMP INTERNATIONAL HOTEL & TOWER** New York City **85.25**

64 **TETON MOUNTAIN LODGE & SPA** Jackson Hole, Wyoming **85.24** ★

65 **RITZ-CARLTON, BACHELOR GULCH** Beaver Creek, Colorado **85.21**

66 **PENINSULA NEW YORK** New York City **85.21**

67 **LODGE AT PEBBLE BEACH** California **85.16**

68 **BEVERLY HILLS HOTEL & BUNGALOWS 85.09**

69 **MONTAGE** Laguna Beach, California **85.09**

70 **ENCHANTMENT RESORT** Sedona, Arizona **85.05**

71 **RITZ-CARLTON** Half Moon Bay, California **85.01**

72 **WYNN** Las Vegas **84.97** ★

73 **FOUR SEASONS HOTEL LOS ANGELES AT
BEVERLY HILLS 84.96**

74 **PONTE VEDRA INN & CLUB** Florida **84.94**

75 **MONMOUTH PLANTATION** Natchez, Mississippi **84.89**

76 **L'AUBERGE CARMEL** Carmel-by-the-Sea, California **84.87**

77 **FAIRMONT CHÂTEAU LAKE LOUISE** Alberta **84.87**

78 **FOUR SEASONS RESORT, AVIARA** North San Diego **84.80**

79 **HOTEL BEL-AIR** Los Angeles **84.79**

80 **RITZ-CARLTON, CENTRAL PARK** New York City **84.79**

81 **MANDARIN ORIENTAL** New York City **84.77**

82 **LODGE AT TORREY PINES** La Jolla, California **84.76** ★

83 **WHITE BARN INN & SPA** Kennebunkport, Maine **84.55**

84 **AMERICAN CLUB** Kohler, Wisconsin **84.50**

85 **FOUR SEASONS HOTEL** Philadelphia **84.49**

86 **RITZ-CARLTON** Amelia Island, Florida **84.46**

87 **WHEATLEIGH** Lenox, Massachusetts **84.29**

88 **WINDSOR COURT HOTEL** New Orleans **84.28**

89 **INN BY THE SEA** Cape Elizabeth, Maine **84.27** ★

90 **SONNENALP RESORT OF VAIL** Colorado **84.20**

91 **RITZ-CARLTON, ORLANDO** Grande Lakes, Florida **84.11**

92 **WEDGEWOOD HOTEL & SPA** Vancouver **84.09**

93 **INN OF THE ANASAZI, A ROSEWOOD RESORT**
Santa Fe, New Mexico **84.08**

94 **MANDARIN ORIENTAL** San Francisco **84.07**

95 **RITTENHOUSE HOTEL** Philadelphia **84.04**

96 **HÔTEL PLAZA ATHÉNÉE** New York City **84.02**

97 **TOWNSEND HOTEL** Birmingham, Michigan **83.96**

98 **INN AT PERRY CABIN** St. Michaels, Maryland **83.95**

99 **THE HAY-ADAMS** Washington, D.C. **83.95**

100 **FAIRMONT VANCOUVER AIRPORT 83.91** ★

TOP 25 HOTEL SPAS UNITED STATES + CANADA

1   FOUR SEASONS RESORT Jackson Hole, Wyoming **91.76**
2   SANCTUARY AT KIAWAH ISLAND GOLF RESORT
    South Carolina **91.02**
3   ENCHANTMENT RESORT, MII AMO Sedona, Arizona **90.85**
4   LODGE AT PEBBLE BEACH California **90.49**
5   ROSEWOOD CRESCENT HOTEL Dallas **90.44**
6   MANDARIN ORIENTAL New York **90.28**
7   RITZ-CARLTON, HUNTINGTON HOTEL & SPA
    Pasadena, California **90.13**
8   MANDARIN ORIENTAL Miami **90.07**
9   THE EQUINOX Manchester, Vermont **89.87**
10 PENINSULA BEVERLY HILLS **89.49**
11 AUBERGE DU SOLEIL Rutherford, California **89.06**
12 FOUR SEASONS HOTEL Las Vegas **88.96**
13 DELANO Miami **88.75**
14 BLACKBERRY FARM Walland, Tennessee **88.60**
15 AMERICAN CLUB Kohler, Wisconsin **88.34**
16 FOUR SEASONS RESORT, AVIARA North San Diego **88.11**
17 BOULDERS RESORT & GOLDEN DOOR SPA
    Scottsdale, Arizona **87.94**
18 GROVE PARK INN RESORT & SPA Asheville,
    North Carolina **87.93**
19 RITZ-CARLTON Sarasota **87.85**
20 BEAU RIVAGE RESORT & CASINO Biloxi, Mississippi **87.77**
21 JW MARRIOTT CAMELBACK INN RESORT & SPA
    Scottsdale, Arizona **87.67**
22 RITZ-CARLTON LODGE, REYNOLDS PLANTATION
    Greensboro, Georgia **87.30**
23 ST. REGIS RESORT Aspen **87.25**
24 THE GREENBRIER White Sulphur Springs, West Virginia **87.22**
25 FAIRMONT BANFF SPRINGS Alberta **87.21**

The gatehouse at Boulders Resort & Golden Door Spa, in Scottsdale, Arizona.

TOP 10 HOTEL SPAS HAWAII

1   FOUR SEASONS RESORT HUALALAI Hawaii **92.89**
2   HALEKULANI Oahu **92.19**
3   MAUNA LANI RESORT & BUNGALOWS Hawaii **90.07**
4   FOUR SEASONS RESORT MAUI AT WAILEA **87.50**
5   GRAND WAILEA RESORT HOTEL & SPA Maui **87.08**
6   GRAND HYATT KAUAI RESORT & SPA **86.15**
7   RITZ-CARLTON, KAPALUA Maui **85.91**
8   FAIRMONT KEA LANI Maui **85.16**
9   FAIRMONT ORCHID Hawaii **85.00**
10 JW MARRIOTT IHILANI RESORT & SPA Oahu **84.51**

HAWAII
TOP 25 HOTELS

1. FOUR SEASONS RESORT HUALALAI Hawaii 92.65
2. HALEKULANI Honolulu, Oahu 90.29
3. FOUR SEASONS RESORT MAUI AT WAILEA 89.72
4. FOUR SEASONS RESORT LANAI, THE LODGE AT KOELE 89.29
5. FOUR SEASONS RESORT LANAI AT MANELE BAY* 88.86
6. FAIRMONT KEA LANI Maui 87.62
7. MAUNA LANI BAY HOTEL & BUNGALOWS Hawaii 87.13
8. HOTEL HANA-MAUI & HONUA SPA Maui 87.04
9. KAHALA HOTEL & RESORT Honolulu, Oahu 84.14
10. GRAND HYATT KAUAI RESORT & SPA 83.20
11. GRAND WAILEA RESORT HOTEL & SPA Maui 83.00
12. RITZ-CARLTON, KAPALUA Maui 82.21
13. ROYAL HAWAIIAN Honolulu, Oahu 81.91
14. FAIRMONT ORCHID Hawaii 81.77
15. HAPUNA BEACH PRINCE HOTEL Hawaii 81.76
16. PRINCEVILLE RESORT Kauai 81.28
17. HYATT REGENCY MAUI RESORT & SPA 80.78
18. JW MARRIOTT IHILANI RESORT & SPA Oahu 80.49
19. WESTIN MAUI RESORT & SPA 78.70
20. MAUI PRINCE HOTEL 78.68
21. HILTON HAWAIIAN VILLAGE BEACH RESORT & SPA Honolulu, Oahu 78.37
22. KONA VILLAGE RESORT Hawaii 77.80
23. SHERATON MAUI RESORT 77.72
24. HILTON WAIKOLOA VILLAGE Hawaii 77.67
25. HYATT REGENCY WAIKIKI RESORT & SPA Oahu 77.55

* Formerly Manele Bay Hotel, Lanai.

A Sea Ranch cottage overlooking the Pacific, at the Hotel Hana-Maui & Honua Spa.

MEXICO+ CENTRAL +SOUTH AMERICA

TOP 25 HOTELS

1 **LA CASA QUE CANTA** Zihuatanejo, Mexico **91.28**
2 **FOUR SEASONS HOTEL** Buenos Aires **90.12**
3 **ESPERANZA** Los Cabos, Mexico **89.68**
4 **RITZ-CARLTON** Santiago, Chile **88.86**
5 **ONE & ONLY PALMILLA** Los Cabos, Mexico **88.32**
6 **TURTLE INN** Placencia, Belize **87.86**
7 **ALVEAR PALACE HOTEL** Buenos Aires **87.80**
8 **FOUR SEASONS RESORT COSTA RICA AT PENINSULA PAPAGAYO 87.67**
9 **LAS MAÑANITAS** Cuernavaca, Mexico **87.27**
10 **ROYAL HIDEAWAY PLAYACAR** Playa del Carmen, Mexico **86.79**
11 **LAPA RIOS** Corcovado National Park, Costa Rica **86.75** ★
12 **PARK HYATT** Mendoza, Argentina **86.71**
13 **BLANCANEAUX LODGE** Cayo, Belize **86.50**
14 **TIDES ZIHUATANEJO*** Mexico **86.42**
15 **TIDES RIVIERA MAYA**** Mexico **86.39**
16 **MAROMA RESORT & SPA** Riviera Maya, Mexico **86.33**
17 **FOUR SEASONS RESORT PUNTA MITA** Mexico **86.00**
18 **LODGE AT CHAA CREEK** Cayo, Belize **85.50**
19 **HOTEL MONASTERIO** Cuzco, Peru **85.47**
20 **FOUR SEASONS HOTEL MÉXICO, D.F.** Mexico City **85.03**
21 **HOTEL MUSEO CASA SANTO DOMINGO** Antigua, Guatemala **85.00**
22 **MARQUIS LOS CABOS** Mexico **84.82** ★
23 **LAS VENTANAS AL PARAÍSO** Los Cabos, Mexico **84.69**
24 **LLAO LLAO HOTEL & RESORT** San Carlos de Bariloche, Argentina **84.56**
25 **RITZ-CARLTON** Cancún **84.36**

*Formerly Hotel Villa del Sol, Zihuatanejo, Mexico.

**Formerly Ikal del Mar, Playa del Carmen, Mexico.

TOP 10 HOTEL SPAS MEXICO + CENTRAL + SOUTH AMERICA

1   ESPERANZA Los Cabos, Mexico **89.29**
2   FOUR SEASONS RESORT COSTA RICA AT PENINSULA PAPAGAYO **88.62**
3   ROYAL HIDEAWAY PLAYACAR Playa del Carmen, Mexico **87.50**
4   FOUR SEASONS RESORT PUNTA MITA Mexico **86.22**
5   FOUR SEASONS HOTEL Buenos Aires **86.14**
6   LAS VENTANAS AL PARAÍSO Los Cabos, Mexico **85.68**
7   ONE & ONLY PALMILLA Los Cabos, Mexico **84.26**
8   PARADISUS RIVIERA Cancún **84.13**
9   PUEBLO BONITO Los Cabos, Mexico **83.63**
10 RITZ-CARLTON Cancún **81.99**

The cliffside La Casa Que Canta, in Zihuatanejo, Mexico. Opposite: A bartender at the Four Seasons Resort Costa Rica.

CARIBBEAN+ THE BAHAMAS+ BERMUDA

TOP 25 HOTELS

1. **JUMBY BAY, A ROSEWOOD RESORT** Antigua **92.24**
2. **LADERA** St. Lucia **91.34**
3. **JAMAICA INN** Ocho Rios, Jamaica **89.78**
4. **MALLIOUHANA HOTEL & SPA** Anguilla **88.86**
5. **HOTEL SAINT-BARTH ISLE DE FRANCE** St. Bart's **88.81**
6. **EDEN ROCK HOTEL** St. Bart's **88.70**
7. **HORNED DORSET PRIMAVERA** Rincón, Puerto Rico **88.54**
8. **FOUR SEASONS RESORT** Nevis **88.10**
9. **CAP JULUCA** Anguilla **87.88**
10. **CUISINART RESORT & SPA** Anguilla **87.02**
11. **COUPLES SANS SOUCI** Ocho Rios, Jamaica **86.50**
12. **THE REEFS** Bermuda **86.45**
13. **PETER ISLAND RESORT** Peter Island **85.97**
14. **HOTEL GUANAHANI & SPA** St. Bart's **85.81**
15. **RITZ-CARLTON** Grand Cayman **85.45** ★
16. **ROYAL PLANTATION** Ocho Rios, Jamaica **85.28** ★
17. **ROUND HILL HOTEL & VILLAS** Montego Bay, Jamaica **85.21**
18. **BIRAS CREEK RESORT** Virgin Gorda **85.00**
19. **SANDY LANE** St. James, Barbados **84.71**
20. **GRAND LIDO BRACO RESORT & SPA** Runaway Bay, Jamaica **84.40** ★
21. **ONE & ONLY OCEAN CLUB** Paradise Island, Bahamas **83.77**
22. **GRACE BAY CLUB** Providenciales, Turks and Caicos **82.83**
23. **PARROT CAY** Turks and Caicos **82.00**
24. **ROCKHOUSE HOTEL** Negril, Jamaica **81.99** ★
25. **PINK SANDS** Harbour Island, Bahamas **81.67**

TOP 10 HOTEL SPAS CARIBBEAN+ THE BAHAMAS+ BERMUDA

1. COUPLES NEGRIL Jamaica **89.88**
2. PARROT CAY Turks and Caicos **89.82**
3. ROSEWOOD LITTLE DIX BAY Virgin Gorda **88.99**
4. ONE & ONLY OCEAN CLUB Paradise Island, Bahamas **87.28**
5. ROUND HILL HOTEL & VILLAS Montego Bay, Jamaica **87.15**
6. FOUR SEASONS RESORT Nevis **86.35**
7. RITZ-CARLTON Grand Cayman **86.14**
8. COUPLES SANS SOUCI Ocho Rios, Jamaica **84.72**
9. CUISINART RESORT & SPA Anguilla **83.87**
10. RITZ-CARLTON GOLF & SPA RESORT Rose Hall, Jamaica **82.84**

A lounge at Parrot Cay, in Turks and Caicos. Below: Poolside daybeds at Grace Bay Club, in Turks and Caicos. Opposite: A guest room at the Hotel Guanahani, on St. Bart's.

EUROPE
TOP 50 HOTELS

1   FOUR SEASONS HOTEL ISTANBUL AT SULTANAHMET 93.55
2   MILESTONE HOTEL London 93.06 ★
3   IL FALCONIERE Cortona, Italy 92.97
4   MANDARIN ORIENTAL Munich 92.73 ★
5   CHÂTEAU LES CRAYÈRES Reims, France 92.39
6   FOUR SEASONS HOTEL GRESHAM PALACE Budapest 92.15
7   LE SIRENUSE Positano, Italy 91.18
8   FOUR SEASONS HOTEL Prague 91.07
9   FOUR SEASONS HOTEL GEORGE V Paris 91.05
10   41 London 90.68 ★
11   IL PELLICANO Porto Ercole, Italy 89.64 ★
12   HÔTEL D'EUROPE Avignon, France 89.42
13   CHÂTEAU DE LA CHÈVRE D'OR Èze Village, France 89.35
14   HÔTEL HERMITAGE Monte Carlo 89.14
15   LA BASTIDE DE MOUSTIERS Moustiers-Ste.-Marie,
     France 89.04
16   DOMAINE DES HAUTS DE LOIRE Onzain, France 89.00
17   HÔTEL DU CAP EDEN-ROC Antibes, France 88.89
18   IL SAN PIETRO Positano, Italy 88.82
19   RITZ-CARLTON Istanbul 88.60 ★
20   BEAU-RIVAGE PALACE Lausanne, Switzerland 88.57
21   HOTEL VILLA CIPRIANI Asolo, Italy 88.27
22   HOTEL HASSLER Rome 88.18
23   GLENEAGLES HOTEL Auchterarder, Scotland 88.18
24   KATIKIES HOTEL Santorini, Greece 88.17 ★
25   RITZ-CARLTON Berlin 88.17 ★
26   GRAVETYE MANOR HOTEL West Sussex, England 87.92
27   VICTORIA-JUNGFRAU GRAND HOTEL & SPA
     Interlaken, Switzerland 87.89
28   THE GORING London 87.50
29   LA COLOMBE D'OR HOTEL St.-Paul-de-Vence, France 87.50
30   L'OUSTAU DE BAUMANIÈRE Les-Baux-de-Provence,
     France 87.27
31   HÔTEL PLAZA ATHÉNÉE Paris 87.26
32   CAPRI PALACE HOTEL & SPA Italy 87.13
33   SAN CLEMENTE PALACE HOTEL & RESORT Venice 86.49 ★
34   LE MEURICE Paris 86.33
35   INTERCONTINENTAL CARLTON Cannes, France 86.31
36   GRAND HOTEL TIMEO Taormina, Italy 86.24 ★
37   PALAZZO SASSO Ravello, Italy 86.24
38   HOTEL SANTA CATERINA Amalfi, Italy 86.14
39   BRENNER'S PARK-HOTEL & SPA Baden-Baden,
     Germany 86.11
40   ST. REGIS GRAND HOTEL Rome 86.09
41   THE RITZ Paris 86.08
42   BAUER IL PALAZZO Venice 86.06
43   GRAND HOTEL QUISISANA Capri, Italy 85.99
44   BAUR AU LAC Zürich 85.98
45   HOTEL IMPERIAL Vienna 85.92
46   WATERFORD CASTLE HOTEL & GOLF CLUB Waterford,
     Ireland 85.90
47   FOUR SEASONS HOTEL London 85.81
48   VILLA SAN MICHELE Fiesole, Italy 85.74
49   VILLA D'ESTE Cernobbio, Italy 85.71
50   ADARE MANOR HOTEL & GOLF RESORT Adare, Ireland 85.58

A sitting area in the Ritz Paris's Coco Chanel suite, above. Opposite: The front entrance of the San Clemente Palace, in Venice.

TOP 5 HOTEL SPAS EUROPE

1   FOUR SEASONS HOTEL GEORGE V Paris 89.02
2   LE SIRENUSE Positano, Italy 88.13
3   VILLA D'ESTE Cernobbio, Italy 82.14
4   BRENNER'S PARK-HOTEL & SPA Baden-Baden, Germany 80.15
5   WESTIN EXCELSIOR Rome 75.00

AFRICA + THE MIDDLE EAST

TOP 25 HOTELS

1 **SINGITA SABI SAND/KRUGER NATIONAL PARK**
   South Africa **94.30**
2 **SABI SABI PRIVATE GAME RESERVE** Sabi Sands,
   South Africa **92.81**
3 **MOMBO CAMP** Moremi Game Reserve, Botswana **92.08**
4 **FOUR SEASONS HOTEL CAIRO AT NILE PLAZA 92.00**
5 **CAPE GRACE** Cape Town **91.52**
6 **MALAMALA GAME RESERVE** Mpumalanga, South Africa **91.38**
7 **KICHWA TEMBO** Masai Mara, Kenya **91.25**
8 **NGORONGORO CRATER LODGE** Tanzania **91.11**
9 **FOUR SEASONS HOTEL** Amman, Jordan **90.95**
10 **SWEETWATERS TENTED CAMP** Sweetwaters Game Reserve,
   Kenya **90.50**
11 **LONDOLOZI PRIVATE GAME RESERVE** Sabi Sands,
   South Africa **90.19**

12 **FOUR SEASONS HOTEL CAIRO AT THE FIRST RESIDENCE 90.14**
13 **TORTILIS CAMP** Amboseli National Park, Kenya **90.00** ★
14 **KIRAWIRA LUXURY TENTED CAMP** Serengeti National Park,
   Tanzania **89.92**
15 **FAIRMONT MARA SAFARI CLUB** Masai Mara, Kenya **89.87**
16 **JAO CAMP** Moremi Game Reserve, Botswana **89.47** ★
17 **TABLE BAY HOTEL** Cape Town **89.23**
18 **LE QUARTIER FRANÇAIS** Franschhoek, South Africa **89.00** ★
19 **THE WESTCLIFF** Johannesburg **88.68**
20 **MOUNT NELSON HOTEL** Cape Town **87.94**
21 **FAIRMONT MOUNT KENYA SAFARI CLUB** Nanyuki, Kenya **87.46**
22 **AMBOSELI SERENA SAFARI LODGE** Amboseli National Park,
   Kenya **86.82** ★
23 **ROYAL LIVINGSTONE** Livingstone, Zambia **86.69**
24 **CHOBE CHILWERO** Chobe National Park, Botswana **85.87**
25 **NGORONGORO SERENA SAFARI LODGE** Tanzania **85.78**

Cape Town's Cape
Grace hotel, with
Table Mountain in the
background. Opposite:
A Masai-style cottage
at Ngorongoro Crater
Lodge, in Tanzania.

A sitting area at the Oriental, in Bangkok. Opposite: The main pool at the Four Seasons Resort Chiang Mai.

ASIA
TOP 10 HOTEL SPAS

1   FOUR SEASONS RESORT CHIANG MAI Thailand 95.51
2   THE ORIENTAL Bangkok 94.06
3   JW MARRIOTT PHUKET RESORT & SPA Thailand 93.75
4   FOUR SEASONS RESORT BALI AT JIMBARAN BAY 90.94
5   PENINSULA BANGKOK 90.44
6   OBEROI AMARVILAS Agra, India 90.06
7   RITZ-CARLTON BALI RESORT & SPA 89.93
8   SHANGRI-LA HOTEL Bangkok 88.82
9   PENINSULA HONG KONG 83.75
10 INTERCONTINENTAL Hong Kong 81.48

TOP 50 HOTELS

1. OBEROI UDAIVILAS Udaipur, India 94.36
2. THE ORIENTAL Bangkok 94.23
3. OBEROI AMARVILAS Agra, India 92.56
4. OBEROI RAJVILAS Jaipur, India 92.50
5. PENINSULA BANGKOK 92.41
6. FOUR SEASONS RESORT CHIANG MAI Thailand 91.90
7. RITZ-CARLTON MILLENIA Singapore 90.59
8. THE STRAND Yangon, Myanmar 90.56 ★
9. PENINSULA HONG KONG 90.37
10. RAFFLES HOTEL Singapore 90.15
11. FOUR SEASONS HOTEL Bangkok 89.93
12. FOUR SEASONS RESORT BALI AT JIMBARAN BAY 88.83
13. FULLERTON HOTEL Singapore 88.61
14. SHANGRI-LA'S FAR EASTERN PLAZA HOTEL Taipei 88.59
15. TAJ LAKE PALACE Udaipur, India 88.55
16. FOUR SEASONS HOTEL Hong Kong 88.50
17. SHANGRI-LA HOTEL Bangkok 88.28
18. FOUR SEASONS HOTEL Singapore 88.24
19. FOUR SEASONS HOTEL Shanghai 88.08
20. PENINSULA BEIJING 87.87
21. AMANPURI Phuket, Thailand 87.86
22. THE IMPERIAL New Delhi 87.19
23. RAFFLES GRAND HOTEL D'ANGKOR Siem Reap, Cambodia 86.80
24. THE CONRAD Bangkok 86.76
25. JW MARRIOTT PHUKET RESORT & SPA Thailand 86.39
26. ST. REGIS HOTEL Shanghai 86.32

27. LANGHAM HOTEL Hong Kong 85.90 ★
28. INTERCONTINENTAL Hong Kong 85.69
29. BANYAN TREE Phuket, Thailand 85.50
30. SOFITEL METROPOLE Hanoi 85.47
31. FOUR SEASONS HOTEL TOKYO AT CHINZAN-SO 85.45
32. THE REGENT Shanghai 85.39 ★
33. RAFFLES HOTEL LE ROYAL Phnom Penh, Cambodia 85.37
34. JW MARRIOTT HOTEL Bangkok 85.32
35. GRAND HYATT ERAWAN Bangkok 85.18
36. MANDARIN ORIENTAL Kuala Lumpur 85.12
37. EVASON ANA MANDARA RESORT & SIX SENSES SPA
    Nha Trang, Vietnam 85.05
38. RITZ-CARLTON BALI RESORT & SPA 85.00
39. PARK HYATT SAIGON Ho Chi Minh City, Vietnam 84.88 ★
40. MANDARIN ORIENTAL Hong Kong 84.82
41. ST. REGIS HOTEL Beijing 84.64
42. PARK HYATT Tokyo 84.50
43. FAIRMONT SINGAPORE* 84.25
44. MANDARIN ORIENTAL DHARA DHEVI Chiang Mai, Thailand 84.19
45. ISLAND SHANGRI-LA Hong Kong 84.17
46. JW MARRIOTT HOTEL SHANGHAI AT TOMORROW SQUARE 84.03★
47. KOWLOON SHANGRI-LA Hong Kong 83.51
48. ROYAL ORCHID SHERATON HOTEL & TOWERS Bangkok 83.04
49. WESTIN BUND CENTER Shanghai 83.01 ★
50. PUDONG SHANGRI-LA Shanghai 82.84

*Formerly Raffles the Plaza, Singapore

AUSTRALIA + NEW ZEALAND + THE SOUTH PACIFIC

Voyages Longitude 131°, near Australia's Ayers Rock, above.
Opposite: An entry hall at Huka Lodge, on New Zealand's North Island.

TOP 25 HOTELS

1   HUKA LODGE Taupo, New Zealand **89.38**
2   OBSERVATORY HOTEL Sydney **87.41**
3   BORA BORA LAGOON RESORT & SPA French Polynesia **87.29**
4   FOUR SEASONS HOTEL Sydney **86.93**
5   HOTEL BORA BORA French Polynesia **85.87**
6   INTERCONTINENTAL Sydney **82.32**
7   LANGHAM HOTEL Melbourne **81.45**
8   PARK HYATT Sydney **81.25**
9   LILIANFELS BLUE MOUNTAINS RESORT & SPA
    Katoomba, Australia **80.48**
10 THE WESTIN Sydney **80.35**
11 SHANGRI-LA HOTEL Sydney **79.98**
12 MILLBROOK Queenstown, New Zealand **79.52**
13 MANTRA TREETOPS RESORT & SPA Port Douglas,
    Australia **79.50** ★

14 PARK HYATT Melbourne **79.41**
15 MOOREA PEARL RESORT & SPA French Polynesia **79.07**
16 SOFITEL Melbourne **78.02**
17 VOYAGES CRADLE MOUNTAIN LODGE Tasmania **77.50**
18 WESTIN DENARAU ISLAND RESORT & SPA
    Fiji **77.17** ★
19 INTERCONTINENTAL RESORT & SPA Moorea,
    French Polynesia **76.97**
20 SHERATON FIJI RESORT Denarau Island, Fiji **76.84**
21 HILTON Auckland **76.23** ★
22 THE GEORGE Christchurch, New Zealand **76.08**
23 GRAND HYATT Melbourne **75.85**
24 KEWARRA BEACH RESORT Cairns, Australia **75.44**
25 VOYAGES LONGITUDE 131° Uluru (Ayers Rock),
    Australia **74.99**

RESOURCES

IN THE FOLLOWING SECTIONS YOU'LL FIND COMPREHENSIVE,
EASY-TO-USE INFORMATION FOR EACH HOTEL, RESORT,
AND SPA FEATURED IN THIS BOOK. IT'S THE ULTIMATE GUIDE
TO WHERE TO GO RIGHT NOW.

A sitting area
near the pool at
Awasi, in Chile.

The approach to
Ca' Zen, in Italy's
Veneto region.

HOTELS DIRECTORY

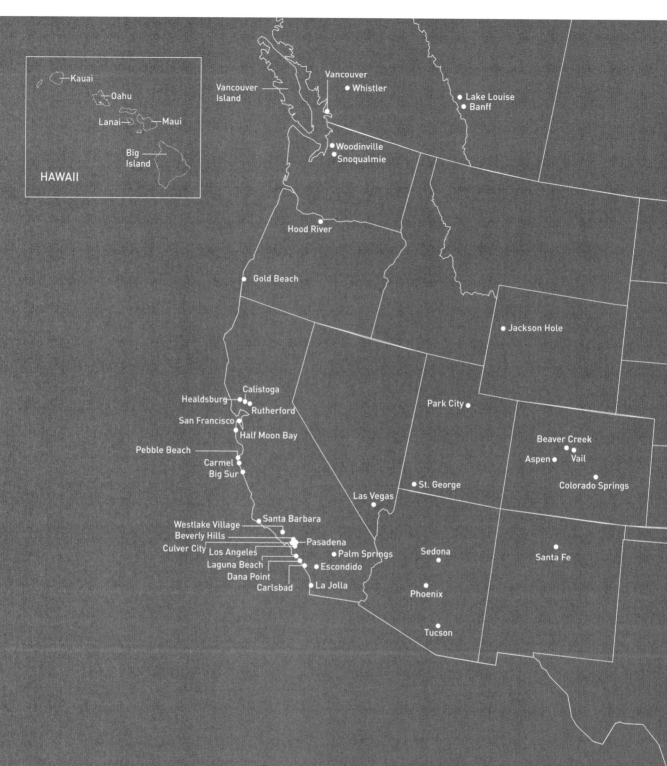

HAWAII

Kauai
Oahu
Lanai — Maui
Big
Island

Vancouver
Island

Vancouver
● Whistler

● Lake Louise
● Banff

● Woodinville
Snoqualmie

Hood River ●

Gold Beach ●

Jackson Hole ●

Calistoga
Healdsburg ●
● Rutherford
San Francisco ●
Half Moon Bay

Pebble Beach
Carmel ●
Big Sur ●

Park City ●

Beaver Creek
Aspen ● ● Vail

St. George ●

Colorado Springs ●

Las Vegas ●

Santa Barbara ●
Westlake Village ●
Beverly Hills ●
Culver City ● Pasadena ●
Los Angeles ● Palm Springs
Laguna Beach ● Escondido
Dana Point ●
Carlsbad ● La Jolla

Sedona ●

Santa Fe ●

Phoenix ●

Tucson ●

UNITED STATES+
CANADA

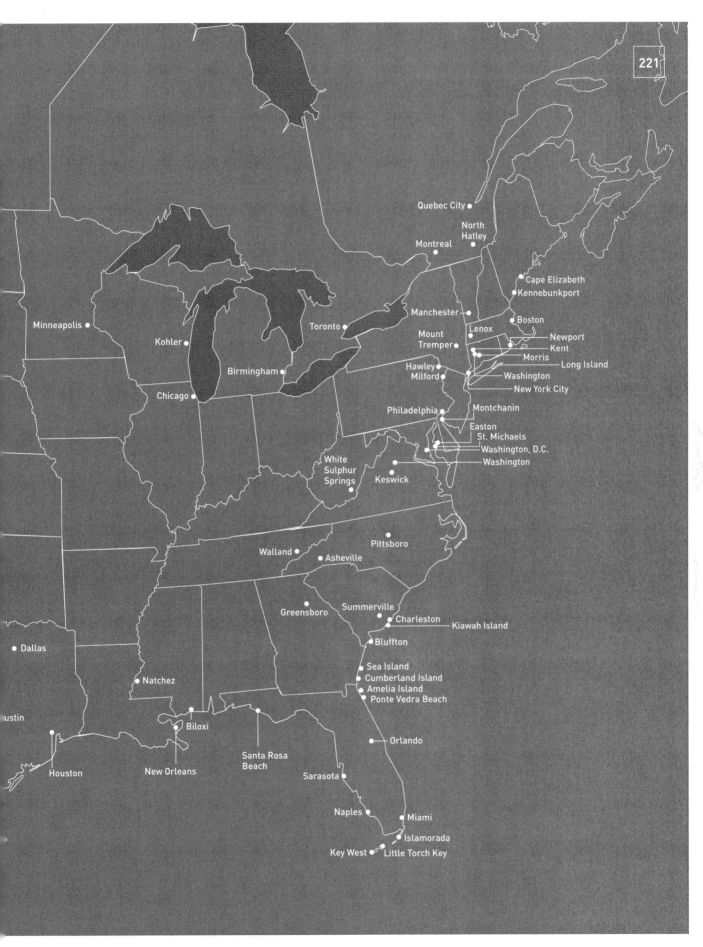

Quebec City

North
Hatley

Montreal

Cape Elizabeth
Kennebunkport

Manchester

Boston

Minneapolis

Toronto

Lenox

Newport
Kent

Kohler

Mount
Tremper

Morris
Long Island

Birmingham

Hawley
Milford

Washington
New York City

Chicago

Philadelphia

Montchanin

Easton
St. Michaels
Washington, D.C.
Washington

White
Sulphur
Springs

Keswick

Pittsboro

Walland

Asheville

Summerville

Greensboro

Charleston
Kiawah Island

Dallas

Bluffton

Natchez

Sea Island
Cumberland Island
Amelia Island
Ponte Vedra Beach

ustin

Orlando

Biloxi

Santa Rosa
Beach

Sarasota

Houston

New Orleans

Naples

Miami

Islamorada

Key West   Little Torch Key

ARIZONA

PHOENIX/SCOTTSDALE
Boulders Resort & Golden Door Spa Luxury adobe villas among a millennia-old rock outcrop. Scottsdale; 866/397-6520 or 480/488-9009; theboulders.com; doubles from $$$

PHOENIX/SCOTTSDALE
Four Seasons Resort Pueblo complex adjacent to a nature preserve. Scottsdale; 800/332-3442 or 480/515-5700; fourseasons.com; doubles from $$

PHOENIX/SCOTTSDALE
Camelback Inn, a JW Marriott Resort & Spa 300 casitas surrounding a historic hotel. Scottsdale; 800/228-9290 or 480/948-1700; camelbackinn.com; doubles from $

SEDONA
Enchantment Resort Adobe-inspired property bordering a national forest and a red-rock box canyon. 800/826-4180 or 928/282-2900; enchantmentresort.com; doubles from $$

TUCSON
Canyon Ranch 150-acre former dude ranch in the Catalina foothills. 800/742-9000 or 520/749-9655; canyonranch.com; doubles from $$$$

TUCSON
Miraval Resort Southwestern casitas on 400 Sonoran Desert acres. 800/232-3969; miraval resort.com; doubles from $$$$, all-inclusive

CALIFORNIA

BIG SUR
Post Ranch Inn Redwood-and-slate cottages on 100 acres overlooking the ocean. 800/527-2200 or 831/667-2200; postranch inn.com; doubles from $$$, including breakfast

BIG SUR
Ventana Inn & Spa Contemporary cedar lodges set 1,200 feet above the Pacific. 800/628-6500 or 831/667-2331; ventanainn.com; doubles from $$$, including breakfast

CARMEL
L'Auberge Carmel Gabled inn built around a landscaped courtyard in the town center. 831/624-8578; lauberge carmel.com; doubles from $$, including breakfast

CARMEL
Bernardus Lodge Mediterranean-style resort surrounded by vineyards, in the Santa Lucia Mountains. 888/648-9463 or 831/658-3400; bernardus.com; doubles from $$$

HALF MOON BAY
Ritz-Carlton Golf and spa resort on an oceanfront cliff 30 miles south of San Francisco. 800/241-3333 or 650/712-7000; ritzcarlton.com; doubles from $$

LOS ANGELES AREA
Beverly Hills Hotel & Bungalows Mission-style hotel on 12 acres of tropical gardens. 9641 Sunset Blvd., Beverly Hills; 800/283-8885 or 310/276-2251; beverlyhillshotel.com; doubles from $$

LOS ANGELES AREA
Culver Hotel Recently restored 1924 hotel steeped in Hollywood history. 9400 Culver Blvd., Culver City; 310/838-7963; culverhotel.com; doubles from $

LOS ANGELES AREA
Four Seasons Hotel Los Angeles at Beverly Hills 16-story tower with traditional interiors, a short walk from Rodeo Drive. 300 S. Doheny Dr., Los Angeles; 800/332-3442 or 310/786-2227; fourseasons.com; doubles from $$

LOS ANGELES AREA
Hotel Bel-Air Storied hideaway amid courtyards and gardens in a residential neighborhood. 701 Stone Canyon Rd., Los Angeles; 800/648-4097 or 310/472-1211; hotelbelair.com; doubles from $$

LOS ANGELES AREA
Langham Huntington Hotel & Spa Luxe landmark overlooking San Marino. Pasadena; 626/568-3900; langhamhotels.com; doubles from $$

LOS ANGELES AREA
Peninsula Beverly Hills Urbane hotel with a luxe French flair. 9882 S. Santa Monica Blvd., Beverly Hills; 800/462-7899 or 310/551-2888; peninsula.com; doubles from $$

NAPA/SONOMA
Auberge du Soleil Mediterranean-style inn on 33 acres of olive groves. Rutherford; 800/348-5406 or 707/963-1211; auberge dusoleil.com; doubles from $$$

NAPA/SONOMA
Calistoga Ranch Shingled cottages tucked into a canyon overlooking the Mayacama Mountains. Calistoga; 800/942-4220 or 707/254-2800; calistoga ranch.com; doubles from $$$

NAPA/SONOMA
Madrona Manor Victorian mansion in historic Dry Creek Valley. Healdsburg;

800/258-4003 or 707/433-4231; madronamanor.com; doubles from $$, including breakfast

ORANGE COUNTY

Montage Laguna Beach Craftsman-style hotel on a bluff overlooking the Pacific. 888/715-6700 or 949/715-6000; montagelagunabeach.com; doubles from $$$$

ORANGE COUNTY

Ritz-Carlton, Laguna Niguel Family-friendly resort in a lively harborside town. Dana Point; 800/241-3333 or 949/240-2000; ritzcarlton.com; doubles from $$

PALM SPRINGS

Orbit In 1950's motel filled with period furniture. 877/996-7248 or 760/323-3585; orbitin.com; doubles from $$

PEBBLE BEACH

Inn at Spanish Bay Contemporary hacienda famed for golf, on the Monterey Peninsula. 800/654-9300 or 831/647-7500; pebblebeach.com; doubles from $$$

PEBBLE BEACH

Lodge at Pebble Beach 1919 Georgian buildings with expansive lawns, above Carmel Bay. 800/654-9300 or 831/647-7500; pebblebeach.com; doubles from $$$

SAN DIEGO AREA

Four Seasons Resort Aviara Spanish-colonial golf resort 30 minutes from San Diego. Carlsbad; 800/332-3442 or 760/603-6800; fourseasons.com; doubles from $$

SAN DIEGO AREA

Golden Door Asian-inspired spa retreat. Escondido; 800/424-0777 or 760/744-5777; goldendoor.com; doubles from $$$$$, all-inclusive

SAN DIEGO AREA

Lodge at Torrey Pines Craftsman-style resort on the 18th fairway of the Torrey Pines Golf Course. La Jolla; 800/656-0087 or 858/453-4420; lodgetorreypines.com; doubles from $$

SAN FERNANDO VALLEY

Four Seasons Hotel 270-room hotel with a medically oriented spa on 9 landscaped acres. Westlake Village; 800/332-3442 or 818/575-3000; fourseasons.com; doubles from $$

SAN FRANCISCO

Campton Place Cozy, business-friendly hotel steps from Union Square. 340 Stockton St.; 866/332-1670 or 415/781-5555; camptonplace.com; doubles from $$$

SAN FRANCISCO

Four Seasons Hotel Polished tower in the Yerba Buena Arts District. 757 Market St.; 800/332-3442 or 415/633-3000; fourseasons.com; doubles from $$

SAN FRANCISCO

Mandarin Oriental Glitzy hotel in the top 11 floors of a Financial District high-rise. 222 Sansome St.; 800/526-6566 or 415/276-9888; mandarinoriental.com; doubles from $$

SAN FRANCISCO

Ritz-Carlton Neoclassical hotel in Nob Hill, close to great shopping and Union Square. 600 Stockton St.; 800/241-3333 or 415/296-7465; ritzcarlton.com; doubles from $$$

SANTA BARBARA

San Ysidro Ranch, A Rosewood Resort Former citrus ranch in the foothills of the Santa Ynez mountains; fresh from a $150 million overhaul. 800/368-6788 or 805/565-1700; rosewood.com; doubles from $$$$

COLORADO

ASPEN

Little Nell Modern ski chalet at the base of Aspen Mountain. 888/843-6355 or 970/920-4600; thelittlenell.com; doubles from $$$$

ASPEN

St. Regis Resort Red-brick compound only 2 blocks from the main gondola. 888/454-9005 or 970/920-3300; stregis.com; doubles from $$$$

BEAVER CREEK

Ritz-Carlton, Bachelor Gulch Exclusive timber lodge with ski-in, ski-out access. 800/241-3333 or 970/748-6200; ritzcarlton.com; doubles from $$$

COLORADO SPRINGS

The Broadmoor Lakeside resort with Italianate interiors, 15 minutes from Pikes Peak. 800/634-7711 or 719/577-5775; broadmoor.com; doubles from $$

VAIL

Sonnenalp Resort of Vail Bavarian-inspired ski chalet with a new $25 million west wing, in the heart of Vail Village. 800/654-8312 or 970/476-5656; sonnenalp.com; doubles from $$$, including breakfast

CONNECTICUT

KENT

Inn at Kent Falls 6-room B&B in an 18th-century farmhouse, steps from the Appalachian Trail. 860/927-3197; theinnatkentfalls.com; doubles from $, including breakfast

MORRIS

Winvian 18 uniquely designed cottages on a pastoral estate. 800/735-2478 or 860/567-9600; winvian.com; doubles from $$$$$, including meals

WASHINGTON

Mayflower Inn & Spa Sophisticated New England retreat with ethereal spa addition. 860/868-9466; mayflowerinn.com; doubles from $$$

DELAWARE

MONTCHANIN

Inn at Montchanin Village Restored 19th-century property in the Brandywine Valley. 800/269-2473 or 302/888-2133; montchanin.com; doubles from $

DISTRICT OF COLUMBIA

WASHINGTON, D.C.

Hay-Adams Italianate hotel across from the White House. 16th and H Sts. NW; 800/424-5054 or 202/638-6600; hayadams.com; doubles from $$$

FLORIDA

AMELIA ISLAND

Ritz-Carlton 8-story tower set between dunes and fairways, 30 minutes from Jacksonville. 800/241-3333 or 904/277-1100; ritzcarlton.com; doubles from $$

FLORIDA KEYS

Casa Morada Airy 16-suite resort 90 minutes south of Miami. Islamorada; 888/881-3030 or 305/664-0044; casamorada.com; doubles from $$

FLORIDA KEYS

Little Palm Island Resort & Spa Thatched-roof bungalows on a private island. Little Torch Key; 800/343-8567 or 305/872-2524; littlepalmisland.com; doubles from $$$$$, including meals

FLORIDA KEYS

Marquesa Hotel 1880's clapboard houses in the historic district. Key West; 800/869-4631 or 305/292-1919; marquesa.com; doubles from $$

MIAMI AREA

Delano Chic Art Deco outpost with a rooftop spa in South Beach. 305/672-2000; delano-hotel.com; doubles from $$$$

MIAMI AREA

Mandarin Oriental Contemporary high-rise near the business district. 866/888-6780 or 305/913-8383; mandarinoriental.com; doubles from $$$

NAPLES

Ritz-Carlton Elegant buff-colored complex on a 3-mile beach. 800/241-3333 or 239/598-3300; ritzcarlton.com; doubles from $$$

ORLANDO

Ritz-Carlton, Grande Lakes Hotel tower on 500 tropical acres 15 minutes from the theme parks. 800/241-3333 or 407/206-2400; ritzcarlton.com; doubles from $$

PONTE VEDRA BEACH

Lodge & Club at Ponte Vedra Beach Spanish colonial–style hotel on a barrier island. 800/243-4304 or 904/273-9500; pvresorts.com; doubles from $$

PONTE VEDRA BEACH

Ponte Vedra Inn & Club Family-friendly resort on 300 oceanfront acres. 800/234-7842 or 904/285-1111; pvresorts.com; doubles from $$

SANTA ROSA BEACH

WaterColor Inn Beachfront hotel designed by David Rockwell on the Gulf Coast. 866/426-2656 or 850/534-5000; watercolorinn.com; doubles from $$

SARASOTA

Ritz-Carlton Opulent waterfront resort with a beach club on Lido Key. 800/241-3333 or 941/309-2000; ritzcarlton.com; doubles from $$

GEORGIA

CUMBERLAND ISLAND

Greyfield Inn 4-story mansion on a barrier island. 888/241-6408 or 904/261-6408; greyfieldinn.com; doubles from $$, including meals

GREENSBORO

Ritz-Carlton Lodge, Reynolds Plantation Shingled cottages and lodge on 10,000 acres near Atlanta. 800/241-3333 or 706/467-0600; ritzcarlton.com; doubles from $$

SEA ISLAND

The Cloister Mediterranean-inspired grand-dame resort. 800/732-4752 or 912/638-3611; seaisland.com; doubles from $$$

HAWAII

BIG ISLAND

Fairmont Orchid Pair of 6-story buildings on a quiet, sheltered Kohala

Winvian's
Charter Oak
cottage, in
Morris,
Connecticut.

beach. 800/441-1414 or 808/885-2000; fairmont. com; doubles from $$

BIG ISLAND
Four Seasons Resort Hualalai Stylish bungalows on the North Kona coast. 888/332-3442 or 808/325-8000; fourseasons.com; doubles from $$$$

A guest on the grounds of the Hotel Hana-Maui & Honua Spa.

BIG ISLAND
Hapuna Beach Prince Hotel 350-room oceanfront complex with a golf course. 888/977-4623 or 808/880-1111; princeresortshawaii.com; doubles from $$

BIG ISLAND
Hilton Waikoloa Village Splashy resort with 3 giant pools and a $7 million art collection. 800/445-8667 or 808/886-1234; hilton waikoloavillage.com; doubles from $$

BIG ISLAND
Kona Village Resort Luxurious thatched-roof bungalows on Kahuwai Bay. 800/367-5290 or 808/325-5555; konavillage. com; doubles from $$$, including meals

BIG ISLAND
Mauna Lani Bay Hotel & Bungalows Glamorous hotel on 3 miles of secluded Kohala shoreline. 800/367-2323 or 808/885-6622; maunalani.com; doubles from $$

KAUAI
Grand Hyatt Kauai Resort & Spa Sprawling resort with a castaway feel and access to Shipwreck Beach. 800/233-1234 or 808/742-1234; hyatt.com; doubles from $$

KAUAI
Princeville Resort Remote hideaway with unparalleled views of Hanalei Bay. 800/325-3589 or 808/826-9644; princeville.com; doubles from $$$

LANAI
Four Seasons Resort Lanai, The Lodge at Koele Hilltop

manor recently renovated to the tune of $50 million. 800/332-3442 or 808/565-4000; fourseasons.com; doubles from $$

LANAI
Four Seasons Resort Lanai at Manele Bay Asian-influenced resort above Hulopoe Bay. 800/332-3442 or 808/565-2000; foursea sons.com; doubles from $$

MAUI
Fairmont Kea Lani Moorish-style property on Polo Beach in Wailea. 800/441-1414 or 808/875-4100; fairmont.com; doubles from $$

MAUI
Four Seasons Resort Maui at Wailea U-shaped resort with tropical gardens, near one of Maui's finest beaches. 800/332-3442 or 808/874-8000; fourseasons. com; doubles from $$

MAUI
Grand Wailea Resort Hotel & Spa 40-acre property with a lavish spa, on Wailea Beach. 800/888-6100 or 808/875-1234; grandwailea. com; doubles from $$$

MAUI
Hotel Hana-Maui & Honua Spa Secluded plantation house near Hamoa Beach. 800/321-4262 or 808/248-

8211; hotelhanamaui.com; doubles from $$

MAUI

Hyatt Regency Resort & Spa Contemporary 10-story hotel on 40 acres next to Kaanapali Beach. 800/233-1234 or 808/661-1234; hyatt.com; doubles from $$

MAUI

Maui Prince Hotel Oceanfront building with an Asian garden and two Robert Trent Jones–designed golf courses. 888/977-4623 or 808/874-1111; princeresorts hawaii.com; doubles from $$

MAUI

Ritz-Carlton, Kapalua 445-room beachfront resort on a pineapple plantation; a $160 million redo was just completed. 800/262-8440 or 808/669-6200; ritzcarlton.com; doubles from $$$

MAUI

Sheraton Maui Resort Sprawling 510-room property fronting Kaanapali Beach. 888/488-3535 or 808/661-0031; sheraton.com; doubles from $$$

MAUI

Westin Resort & Spa Activity-filled getaway with an enormous water park. 800/228-3000 or 808/667-

2525; starwoodhotels.com; doubles from $$$

OAHU

Halekulani 5 buildings surrounded by garden courtyards in Waikiki. 800/367-2343 or 808/923-2311; halekulani.com; doubles from $$

OAHU

Hilton Hawaiian Village Beach Resort & Spa Self-contained resort on 22 oceanfront Honolulu acres. 800/445-8667 or 808/949-4321; hiltonhawaiianvillage.com; doubles from $$

OAHU

Hyatt Regency Waikiki Resort & Spa 2 centrally located towers near Diamond Head. 800/233-1234 or 808/923-1234; hyatt.com; doubles from $$

OAHU

JW Marriott Ihilani Resort & Spa High-rise with four man-made lagoons in Ko Olina. 800/626-4446 or 808/679-0079; ihilani.com; doubles from $$

OAHU

Kahala Hotel & Resort 10-story oceanfront resort on a pristine beach near Waikiki. 800/367-2525 or 808/739-8888; kahalaresort.com; doubles from $$

OAHU

Royal Hawaiian Iconic, pink 1920's hotel on Waikiki Beach. 866/716-8140 or 808/923-7311; royal-hawaiian.com; doubles from $$

ILLINOIS

CHICAGO

Four Seasons Hotel Polished hotel with unrivaled city views. 120 E. Delaware St.; 800/332-3442 or 312/280-8800; fourseasons.com; doubles from $$$

CHICAGO

Peninsula Chicago Contemporary downtown tower near Michigan Avenue. 108 E. Superior St.; 866/288-8889 or 312/337-2888; peninsula.com; doubles from $$$

CHICAGO

Ritz-Carlton, A Four Seasons Hotel Marble-bedecked hotel occupying 21 floors of Water Tower Place. 160 E. Pearson St.; 800/332-3442 or 312/266-1000; fourseasons.com; doubles from $$

LOUISIANA

NEW ORLEANS

Windsor Court Hotel 23-story granite hotel in the Central Business District. 300 Gravier St.; 800/262-2662 or 504/523-6000;

windsorcourthotel.com; doubles from $$

MAINE

CAPE ELIZABETH

Inn by the Sea Shingled beachfront hotel just south of Portland. 800/888-4287 or 207/799-3134; innbythe sea.com; doubles from $$

KENNEBUNKPORT

White Barn Inn & Spa 19th-century inn along the Kennebunk River. 207/967-2321; whitebarn inn.com; doubles from $$, including breakfast

MARYLAND

EASTON

Inn at 202 Dover 5-room B&B in a restored Chesapeake Bay mansion. 866/450-7600; innat202 dover.com; doubles from $$

ST. MICHAELS

Inn at Perry Cabin 1816 manor on a Chesapeake Bay inlet. 800/722-2949 or 410/745-2200; perrycabin.com; doubles from $$

MASSACHUSETTS

BOSTON

XV Beacon Contemporary hotel in a Beaux-Arts building in quiet Beacon Hill. 15 Beacon St.; 877/982-3226 or 617/670-1500; xvbeacon.com; doubles from $$$

BOSTON
Four Seasons Hotel Red-brick hotel facing the Public Garden. 200 Boylston St.; 800/332-3442 or 617/338-4400; fourseasons.com; doubles from $$$

LENOX
Canyon Ranch Exclusive spa in a restored mansion. 800/742-9000 or 413/637-4100; canyonranch.com; doubles from $$$$, all-inclusive

LENOX
Blantyre Tudor-style manor on 117 acres in the Berkshires. 800/735-2478 or 413/637-3556; blantyre. com; doubles from $$$

LENOX
Wheatleigh 1893 palazzo with museum-quality art, minutes from Tanglewood. 413/637-0610; wheatleigh. com; doubles from $$$

MICHIGAN
BIRMINGHAM
Townsend Hotel European-style interiors in a well-heeled Detroit suburb. 100 Townsend St.; 800/548-4172 or 248/642-7900; townsend hotel.com; doubles from $$

MINNESOTA
MINNEAPOLIS
Chambers Hotel David Rockwell–designed

downtown hotel. 901 Hennepin Ave.; 877/767-6990 or 612/767-6900; chambersminneapolis. com; doubles from $$

MISSISSIPPI
BILOXI
Beau Rivage Resort & Casino High-rise complex on the Gulf of Mexico. 888/567-6667 or 228/386-7111; beaurivage.com; doubles from $

NATCHEZ
Monmouth Plantation Greek Revival mansion on 26 acres, 2 miles from the Mississippi River. 800/828-4531 or 601/442-5852; monmouthplantation. com; doubles from $

NEVADA
LAS VEGAS
Bellagio Italianate resort with a man-made lake on the Strip. 3600 Las Vegas Blvd. S.; 888/987-6667 or 702/693-7111; bellagio.com; doubles from $$

LAS VEGAS
Four Seasons Hotel Recently revamped property on floors 35–39 of the Mandalay Bay tower. 3960 Las Vegas Blvd. S.; 800/332-3442 or 702/632-5000; fourseasons.com; doubles from $$

LAS VEGAS
Wynn Las Vegas Resort & Country Club Posh hotel on the Strip hidden behind a man-made mountain. 3131 Las Vegas Blvd. S.; 888/320-9966 or 702/770-7000; wynnlasvegas.com; doubles from $$$

NEW MEXICO
SANTA FE
Inn of the Anasazi, A Rosewood Hotel Pueblo hotel filled with artifacts steps from the main plaza. 113 Washington Ave.; 800/688-8100 or 505/988-3030; innoftheanasazi.com; doubles from $$

NEW YORK
LONG ISLAND
Shinn Estate Farmhouse 4-room North Fork B&B set on its own vineyard. 631/804-0367; shinnfarmhouse. com; doubles from $

MOUNT TREMPER
Kate's Lazy Meadow Retro-chic Catskills motel on 9 acres. 845/688-7200; lazymeadow.com; doubles from $

NEW YORK CITY
Bowery Hotel 135-room hotel with a boho vibe and a popular restaurant. 335 Bowery; 212/505-9100; theboweryhotel.com; doubles from $$$

NEW YORK CITY
Four Seasons Hotel Sleek I. M. Pei–designed tower in midtown. 57 E. 57th St.; 800/332-3442 or 212/758-5700; fourseasons.com; doubles from $$$$$

NEW YORK CITY
Hôtel Plaza Athénée Upper East Side landmark building on a quiet street. 37 E. 64th St.; 800/447-8800 or 212/734-9100; plaza-athenee. com; doubles from $$$

NEW YORK CITY
The Lowell Intimate 1920's hotel on the Upper East Side. 28 E. 63rd St.; 800/221-4444 or 212/838-1400; lowellhotel.com; doubles from $$$

NEW YORK CITY
Mandarin Oriental High-rise hotel with Central Park views. 80 Columbus Circle; 866/526-6567 or 212/805-8800; mandarinoriental. com; doubles from $$$$

NEW YORK CITY
Peninsula New York 1905 Beaux-Arts building near Central Park. 700 Fifth Ave.; 800/262-9467 or 212/956-2888; peninsula.com; doubles from $$$$

NEW YORK CITY
Ritz-Carlton, Battery Park Art Deco–inspired hotel

A guest room at 6 Columbus, in New York City.

in the Financial District. 2 West St.; 800/241-3333 or 212/344-0800; ritzcarlton.com; doubles from $$$$

NEW YORK CITY
Ritz-Carlton, Central Park 22-floor hotel with classic interiors, on Central Park South. 50 Central Park S.; 800/241-3333 or 212/380-9100; ritzcarlton.com; doubles from $$$$

NEW YORK CITY
6 Columbus Stylish 1960's-inspired hotel, across from the Time Warner Center. 6 Columbus Circle; 877/626-5862 or 212/204-3000; thompsonhotels.com; doubles from $$

NEW YORK CITY
St. Regis Recently renovated 1904 Beaux-Arts landmark in Midtown East. 2 E. 55th St.; 800/759-7550 or 212/753-4500; stregis.com; doubles from $$$$

NEW YORK CITY
Trump International Hotel & Tower Hotel occupying floors 3–17 of a 52-story Philip Johnson-designed tower on Columbus Circle. 1 Central Park West; 888/448-7867 or 212/299-1000; trumpintl.com; doubles from $$$

NORTH CAROLINA
ASHEVILLE
Grove Park Inn Resort & Spa Historic Arts-and-Crafts hotel with views of the Blue Ridge Mountains. 800/438-5800 or 828/252-2711; groveparkinn.com; doubles from $$

ASHEVILLE
Inn on Biltmore Estate Manor house on George Vanderbilt's Biltmore estate. 800/858-4130 or 828/225-1600; biltmore.com; doubles from $$

ASHEVILLE
Richmond Hill Inn 1889 mansion and 9 cottages in the Blue Ridge Mountains. 800/545-9238 or 828/252-7313; richmondhillinn.com; doubles from $, including breakfast

PITTSBORO
Fearrington House Country Inn Refined inn on an 18th-century farm near Raleigh-Durham. 800/277-0130 or 919/542-2121; fearrington.com; doubles from $$

OREGON
GOLD BEACH
Tu Tu' Tun Lodge Craftsman-style lodge on the Rogue River. 800/864-6357 or 541/247-6664; tututun.com; doubles from $

HOOD RIVER
Columbia Gorge Hotel 1921 villa on one of the country's widest stretches of river. 800/345-1921 or 541/386-5566; columbiagorgehotel.com; doubles from $

PENNSYLVANIA
HAWLEY
Lodge at Woodloch Rustic-chic retreat on 75 wooden acres. 866/953-8500 or 570/685-8500; thelodgeatwoodloch.com; doubles from $$$

MILFORD
Hotel Fauchère Historic 1880 inn, fresh from a 5-year renovation. 570/409-1212; hotelfauchere.com; doubles from $$

PHILADELPHIA
Four Seasons Hotel Refined hotel with Federal-style furnishings on Logan Square. 1 Logan Sq.; 800/332-3442 or 215/963-1500; fourseasons.com; doubles from $$

PHILADELPHIA
Rittenhouse Hotel 9 floors of a 33-story building on a pretty, tranquil city square. 210 W. Rittenhouse Sq.; 800/635-1042 or 215/546-9000; rittenhousehotel.com; doubles from $$

RHODE ISLAND
NEWPORT
Castle Hill Inn & Resort Victorian manse on a Narragansett Bay peninsula. 888/466-1355 or 401/849-3800; castlehillinn.com; doubles from $$$, including breakfast

SOUTH CAROLINA
BLUFFTON
Inn at Palmetto Bluff Low-country resort on 22,000 acres, 30 minutes from Hilton Head. 866/706-6565 or 843/706-6500; palmettobluffresort.com; doubles from $$$$

CHARLESTON
Planters Inn Elegant 1844 town house in the historic district. 112 N. Market St.; 800/845-7082 or 843/722-2345; plantersinn.com; doubles from $$

CHARLESTON
Wentworth Mansion Restored 1886 residence with Tiffany windows and azalea gardens. 149 Wentworth St.; 888/466-1886 or 843/853-1886; wentworthmansion.com; doubles from $$

KIAWAH ISLAND
Sanctuary at Kiawah Island Golf Resort Barrier-island estate 30 minutes from Charleston. 877/683-1234

or 843/768-6000; the
sanctuary.com; doubles
from $$

SUMMERVILLE
Woodlands Resort & Inn
Greek Revival mansion on
42 acres near Charleston.
800/774-9999 or 843/875-
2600; woodlandsinn.com;
doubles from $$

TENNESSEE
WALLAND
Blackberry Farm Country
estate in the Great Smoky
Mountains. 800/648-4252
or 865/984-8166; blackberry
farm.com; doubles from
$$$, including meals

TEXAS
AUSTIN
Four Seasons Hotel Luxe
property on 11 lakeside
acres near the convention
center. 98 San Jacinto Blvd.;
800/332-3442 or 512/478-
4500; fourseasons.com;
doubles from $$

AUSTIN
Lake Austin Spa Hill
Country hideaway with
colorful touches. 1705 S.
Quinlan Park Rd., 800/847-
5637 or 512/372-7300; lake
austin.com; doubles from $$

DALLAS
Rosewood Crescent Hotel
Limestone château near the
Arts District. 400 Crescent

Court. 888/767-3966 or 214/
871-3200; crescentcourt.
com; doubles from $$$

HOUSTON
Hotel Icon 135-room downtown hotel in a landmark
1911 building. 220 Main St.;
800/970-4266 or 713/224-
4266; hotelicon.com;
doubles from $

UTAH
PARK CITY
Stein Eriksen Lodge Chalet
with stone fireplaces at Deer
Valley ski resort. 800/453-
1302 or 435/649-3700; stein
lodge.com; doubles from $$$

ST. GEORGE
Green Valley Spa & Resort
Family-owned outpost near
Zion National Park. 800/
237-1068 or 435/628-8060;
greenvalleyspa.com;
doubles from $$

ST. GEORGE
Red Mountain Spa Adobe-
inspired resort surrounded
by red-rock canyons. 800/
407-3002 or 435/673-4905;
redmountainspa.com;
doubles from $$$

VERMONT
MANCHESTER VILLAGE
The Equinox Cozy 1769 inn
in a classic New England
village. 800/362-4747 or
802/362-4700; equinox
resort.com; doubles from $$

VIRGINIA
KESWICK
Keswick Hall Genteel
country estate with a golf
course. 800/274-5391 or
434/979-3440; keswick.com;
doubles from $$

WASHINGTON
Inn at Little Washington
Antiques-filled house near

the Shenandoah Valley.
540/675-3800; theinnatlittle
washington.com; doubles
from $$$, including
breakfast

WASHINGTON
SNOQUALMIE
Salish Lodge & Spa
Contemporary chalet atop
the 268-foot Snoqualmie

**A cottage deck at
Castle Hill Inn &
Resort, in Newport,
Rhode Island.**

Falls in the foothills of the Cascade Mountains. 800/272-5474 or 425/888-2556; salishlodge.com; doubles from $$

WOODINVILLE
Willows Lodge Rustic wine-country retreat 20 minutes northeast of Seattle. 877/424-3930 or 425/424-3900; willowslodge.com; doubles from $$

WEST VIRGINIA
WHITE SULPHUR SPRINGS
The Greenbrier 1913 resort in the Allegheny Mountains, fresh from a $50 million renovation. 800/624-6070 or 304/536-1110; greenbrier.com; doubles from $$

WISCONSIN
KOHLER
American Club Tudor-style hotel an hour north of Milwaukee. 800/344-2838 or 920/457-8000; destinationkohler.com; doubles from $$

WYOMING
JACKSON HOLE
Four Seasons Resort Contemporary alpine lodge at the base of the Tetons. 800/332-3442 or 307/732-5000; fourseasons.com; doubles from $$$

JACKSON HOLE
Rusty Parrot Lodge & Spa Intimate lodgepole-pine inn across from Miller Park and a short walk to town square. 800/458-2004 or 307/733-2000; rustyparrot.com; doubles from $$, including breakfast

JACKSON HOLE
Teton Mountain Lodge & Spa Family-friendly lodge 1 mile from Grand Teton National Park. 800/801-6615 or 307/734-7111; tetonlodge.com; doubles from $

CANADA
ALBERTA
BANFF
Fairmont Banff Springs Scottish-style manor with a golf course and access to skiing. 800/441-1414 or 403/762-2211; fairmont.com; doubles from $$

LAKE LOUISE
Fairmont Chateau Lake Louise 1890 resort on 20 acres, across from Victoria Glacier. 800/441-1414 or 403/522-3511; fairmont.com; doubles from $$

LAKE LOUISE
Post Hotel & Spa Gracious family-run lodge dating from 1942, on the Pipestone River, 5 minutes from Lake Louise. 800/661-1586 or 403/522-3989; posthotel.com; doubles from $$

BRITISH COLUMBIA
VANCOUVER
Fairmont Vancouver Airport Modern glass tower atop a departures terminal at Vancouver International Airport. 800/441-1414 or 604/207-5200; fairmont.com; doubles from $$

VANCOUVER
Wedgewood Hotel & Spa Downtown art-filled hotel. 845 Hornby St.; 800/663-0666 or 604/689-7777; wedgewoodhotel.com; doubles from $$$

VANCOUVER ISLAND
Sooke Harbour House Clapboard inn on the edge of the Pacific, overlooking the Olympic Mountains. 800/889-9688 or 250/642-3421; sookeharbourhouse.com; doubles from $$, including breakfast

VANCOUVER ISLAND
Wickaninnish Inn Cedar inn with driftwood furnishings on a remote Pacific promontory. 800/333-4604 or 250/725-3100; wickinn.com; doubles from $$

WHISTLER
Four Seasons Resort Luxe forest lodge, a 5-minute walk from Blackcomb. 800/332-3442 or 604/935-3400; fourseasons.com; doubles from $$

ONTARIO
TORONTO
Drake Hotel Eclectic hotel in a burgeoning neighborhood. 1150 Queen St. W.; 866/372-5386 or 416/531-5042; thedrakehotel.ca; doubles from $

QUEBEC
MONTREAL
Hôtel Le St.-James Antiques-filled 19th-century former bank in Vieux Montréal. 355 Rue St. Jacques; 866/841-3111 or 514/841-3111; hotellestjames.com; doubles from $$

NORTH HATLEY
Manoir Hovey Elegant lakeside inn with a renowned restaurant. 800/661-2421 or 819/842-2421; manoirhovey.com; doubles from $$, including breakfast and dinner

QUEBEC CITY
Auberge Saint-Antoine Stylish downtown hotel in a converted 19th-century warehouse. 8 Rue St. Antoine; 888/692-2211 or 418/692-2211; saint-antoine.com; doubles from $

Drake Hotel's café,
in Toronto.

Tecate

Los Cabos

Sayulita

Puerto Vallarta

Yelapa

Zihuatenjo

San Miguel
de Allende

Punta
Mita

Cuernavaca

Mexico City

Puebla

Cayo Cancún

Riviera Maya

Ambergris Cay

Placencia

Antigua

Peninsula Papagayo

Nosara

Corcovado
National Park

Tortuguero

Imbabura

Cotopaxi

Cuzco

San Pedro
de Atacama

Santiago

Mendoza

Colchagua
Valley

Las
Condes

Buenos
Aires

San Miguel
del Monte

Pucón

San
Carlos de
Bariloche

MEXICO+
CENTRAL
+SOUTH
AMERICA

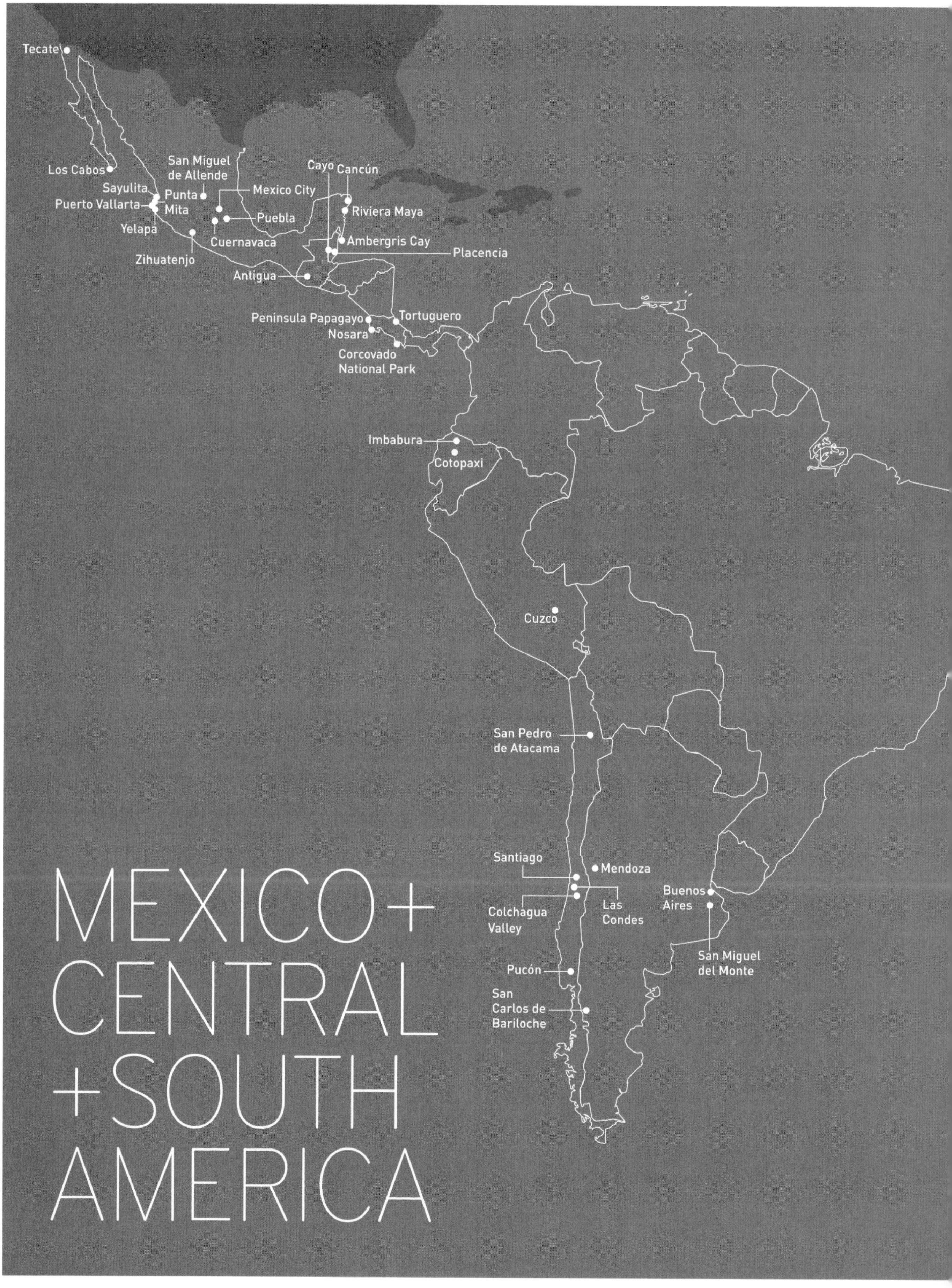

ARGENTINA

BUENOS AIRES

Alvear Palace Hotel 1932 landmark located in the stylish Recoleta district. 1891 Avda. Alvear; 800/223-6800 or 54-11/4808-2100; alvearpalace.com; doubles from $$$

BUENOS AIRES

Four Seasons Hotel Contemporary tower and newly renovated Belle Époque mansion in Recoleta. 1086 Posadas; 800/332-3442 or 54-11/4321-1200; fourseasons. com; doubles from $$

MENDOZA

Park Hyatt Mendoza Hotel Casino & Spa Modern building with restored 19th-century façade, overlooking the Plaza Independencia. 1124 Chile; 888/964-9288 or 54-261/441-1234; parkhyatt. com; doubles from $$

SAN CARLOS DE BARILOCHE

Llao Llao Hotel & Resort, Golf-Spa Historic 1938 lodge in Patagonia's Nahuel Huapi National Park. 54-29/4444-8530; llaollao.com; doubles from $$, including breakfast

SAN MIGUEL DEL MONTE

Candelaria del Monte Country estate in the pampas 90 minutes south of Buenos Aires. 54-2271/442-431; candelariadelmonte.com. ar; doubles from $$, including meals

BELIZE

AMBERGRIS CAY

Matachica Beach Resort 14 thatched roof villas on a reef-fringed island. 011-501/220-5010; matachica.com; doubles from $$

CAYO

Blancaneaux Lodge Resort owned by Francis Ford Coppola near the Mayan ruins of Caracol. 800/746-3743 or 011-501/824-3878; blancaneaux. com; doubles from $$, including breakfast

CAYO

Lodge at Chaa Creek Recently renovated jungle lodge in the foothills of the Maya Mountains. 877/709-8708 or 011-501/824-2037; chaacreek.com; doubles from $$, including breakfast

PLACENCIA

Turtle Inn Balinese-inspired beach cottages, also owned by Francis Ford Coppola. 800/746-3743 or 011-501/523-3244; turtleinn.com; doubles from $$, including breakfast

CHILE

COLCHAGUA VALLEY

Los Lingues Restored 17th-century estate in Chile's main wine-producing region. 56-2/431-0510; loslingues.com; doubles from $

MAIPO VALLEY

Casa Real Hotel European-style manor house on the grounds of the Santa Rita winery. Las Condes; 56-2/821-9966; santarita. com; doubles from $$, including breakfast

SAN PEDRO DE ATACAMA

Awasi 8 adobe bungalows set in the Chilean desert. 888/880-3219 or 56-2/233-9641; awasi.cl; doubles from $$$, all-inclusive

SANTIAGO

Ritz-Carlton Opulent 15-story business hotel in the El Golf district. 15 Calle el Alcalde; 800/241-3333 or 56-2/470-8500; ritzcarlton.com; doubles from $$

VILLARRICA

Hotel Antumalal 1950's retreat surrounded by parkland on the shores of Lake Villarrica. Pucón; 56-45/441-011; antumalal.com; doubles from $

COSTA RICA

CORCOVADO NATIONAL PARK

Lapa Rios Ecolodge Thatched-roof mountainside refuge just outside Corcovado National Park. 011-506/735-5130; laparios. com; doubles from $$, including meals

GUANACASTE

Four Seasons Resort at Peninsula Papagayo Rustic yet refined resort on a secluded peninsula. 800/332-3442 or 011-506/696-0000; fourseasons.com; doubles from $$$

NOSARA

Harmony Hotel Eco-minded hotel and small spa near the beach. 011-506/682-4114; harmonynosara.com; doubles from $$

TORTUGUERO

Tortuga Lodge A pioneering ecotourism destination, accessible only by boat or plane. 011-506/257-0766; costaricaexpeditions.com; doubles from $

ECUADOR

COTOPAXI

Hacienda San Agustín de Callo 11-room inn with Incan details, at the base of a volcano. 593-2/290-6157; incahacienda.com; doubles from $$

IMBABURA

Hacienda Zuleta Family-owned guesthouse on a farm in the Andes. 593-6/266-2182; zuleta.com; doubles from $$$, including meals

GUATEMALA

ANTIGUA

Hotel Museo Casa Santo Domingo Serene hotel in a restored 16th-century convent, a short walk from the town center. 28A Tercera Calle Oriente; 502/7820-1220; casasanto domingo.com.gt; doubles from $

MEXICO

CANCÚN

Paridisus Riviera Seaside property with 494 suites in buildings that resemble *palapas*. 866/436-3542 or 52-998/872-8383; paradisus rivieracancun.com

CANCÚN

Ritz-Carlton Recently renovated Mediterranean-style resort on the beach. 800/241-3333 or 52-998/881-0808; ritzcarlton.com; doubles from $$$

CUERNAVACA

Las Mañanitas Colonial estate in downtown Cuernavaca. 888/413-9199 or 52-777/362-0000; lasmananitas.com.mx;

doubles from $$, including breakfast

LOS CABOS

Esperanza Resort with local touches on a bluff above the Sea of Cortés. Cabo San Lucas; 866/311-2226 or 52-624/145-6400; esperanzare sort.com; doubles from $$$

LOS CABOS

Las Ventanas al Paraíso Sophisticated hideaway along a picturesque stretch of sand. San José del Cabo; 888/767-3966 or 52-624/144-2800; lasventanas.com; doubles from $$$

LOS CABOS

Marquis Los Cabos All-suite beachside resort with a Southwestern feel. San José del Cabo; 877/238-9399 or 52-624/144-2000; marquisloscabos.com; doubles from $$, including breakfast

LOS CABOS

One & Only Palmilla Legendary 1956 hacienda on one of Cabo's few swim-mable beaches. San José del Cabo; 866/552-0001 or 52-624/146-7000; oneand onlypalmilla.com; doubles from $$$

LOS CABOS

Pueblo Bonito 147 suites with patios or balconies

in a whitewashed property. Cabo San Lucas; 800/990-8250 or 52-624/142-9797; pueblobonito.com; doubles from $$

MEXICO CITY

Four Seasons Hotel Elegant 8-story hotel with a desirable downtown address. 500 Paseo de la Reforma; 800/332-3442 or 52-55/5230-1818; fourseasons.com; doubles from $$

PUEBLA

La Purificadora 26-room hotel by architect Ricardo Legorreta. 802 Callejón de la 10 Norte; 52-222/309-1920; lapurificadora.com; doubles from $

PUERTO VALLARTA

Hacienda San Angel Antiques-filled inn with gardens and courtyards, blocks from the waterfront. 877/815-6594 or 52-322/222-2692; haciendasan angel.com; doubles from $$, including breakfast

PUNTA MITA

Four Seasons Resort Recently expanded tiled-roof casita complex on a pristine isthmus outside Puerto Vallarta. 800/332-3442 or 52-329/291-6000; fourseasons.com; doubles from $$$

RIVIERA MAYA

Casa Magna Former vacation estate of drug lord Pablo Escobar, converted into a stylish 22-room resort. 52-998/185-7430; casamagnatulum.com; doubles from $$ per person, including meals

RIVIERA MAYA

Fairmont Mayakoba Eco-friendly golf-and-spa retreat on 50 oceanfront acres. 800/441-1414 or 52-984/206-3000; fairmont.com; doubles from $$

RIVIERA MAYA

Maroma Resort & Spa Modern oasis on a onetime coconut plantation. 866/454-9351 or 52-998/872-8200; maroma hotel.com; doubles from $$$, including breakfast

RIVIERA MAYA

Maya Tulum Wellness Retreat Thatched-roof complex along a strip of white sand. 888/515-4580; mayatulum.com; doubles from $

RIVIERA MAYA

Royal Hideaway Playacar Colonial-style resort with extensive activities. 800/999-9182 or 52-984/873-4500; royalhideaway.com; doubles from $$, all-inclusive

KEY TO THE PRICE ICONS **$** UNDER $250 **$$** $250–$499 **$$$** $500–$749 **$$$$** $750–$999 **$$$$$** $1,000 AND UP

RIVIERA MAYA
The Tides Luxe eco-conscious refuge with 30 villas, surrounded by tropical jungle. 800/332-1672 or 52-984/877-3000; tidesrivieramaya.com; doubles from $$$

SAN MIGUEL DE ALLENDE
The Oasis Stylish 4-room B&B in a restored 17th-century mansion, with fantastic city views. 210/745-1457 or 52-415/154-9850; oasissanmiguel.com; doubles from $$, including breakfast

SAYULITA
Petit Hotel d'Hafa Quirky and charming 6-room hotel in a sleepy Pacific coast surf town. 52-329/291-3806; sayulitalife.com; doubles from $

TECATE
Rancho La Puerta Folk art–filled casitas on a 3,000-acre nature preserve. 877/440-7778 or 858/764-5500; rancholapuerta.com; doubles from $$$$, all-inclusive

YELAPA
Verana Secluded hillside getaway overlooking the Bay of Banderas. 800/530-7176 or 310/360-0155; verana.com; doubles from $$

ZIHUATANEJO
La Casa Que Canta Cliff-hugging retreat above Zihuatanejo Bay. 888/523-5050 or 52-755/555-7000; lacasaquecanta.com; doubles from $$

ZIHUATANEJO
The Tides 72-room adobe resort on a quiet Pacific beach. 866/905-9560 or 52-755/555-5500; tides zihuatanejo.com; doubles from $$$

PERU

CUZCO
Hotel Monasterio Monastery converted into an elegant hotel, in the middle of town. 136 Palacios; 800/237-1236 or 51-84/241-777; monasterio hotel.com; doubles from $$

A patio at Casa Magna, on Mexico's Riviera Maya.

Bermuda

GREAT SOUND

ATLANTIC OCEAN

The Bahamas

ATLANTIC OCEAN

Turks and Caicos

Dominican Republic

Cayman Islands

Jamaica

Puerto Rico

Virgin Gorda

Anguilla

St. Bart's

Nevis

Antigua

Peter Island

Dominica

St. Lucia

Barbados

CARIBBEAN SEA

CARIBBEAN + THE BAHAMAS + BERMUDA

ANGUILLA

Cap Juluca 18 whitewashed Moorish-inspired villas on 179 acres of secluded beachfront. 888/858-5822 or 264/497-6666; capjuluca. com; doubles from $$$$, including breakfast and activities

ANGUILLA

CuisinArt Resort & Spa Mediterranean-style retreat along a stunning coastal stretch. 800/943-3210 or 264/498-2000; cuisinart resort.com; doubles from $$$, including breakfast

ANGUILLA

Malliouhana Hotel & Spa Classic resort set above Meads Bay with a notable spa and Michelin-starred restaurant. 800/835-0796 or 264/497-6111; malliouhana. com; doubles from $$$$

ANTIGUA

Jumby Bay Hideaway on a 300-acre private island. 888/767-3966 or 268/ 462-6000; rosewoodhotels. com; doubles from $$$$$, including meals

BAHAMAS

The Cove at Atlantis High-design rooms with spectacular ocean views in a sophisticated resort within the larger Atlantis complex. 877/268-3847 or 954/809-2100; atlantis.com; doubles from $$$

BAHAMAS

Kamalame Cay Secluded cottages on a barrier island off the eastern coast of Andros. 800/790-7971 or 242/368-6281; kamalame. com; doubles from $$$$

BAHAMAS

One & Only Ocean Club at Paradise Island Refined oceanside estate with a Versailles-inspired garden. 800/321-3000 or 242/ 363-2501; oneandonly resorts.com; doubles from $$$$

BAHAMAS

Pink Sands 20-acre haven of white bungalows, recently redesigned by Barbara Hulanicki. 800/407-4776 or 242/333-2030; pinksandsresort.com; doubles from $$$$

BARBADOS

Sandy Lane Luxurious coral-stone property on a 1,000-foot stretch of white sand. 866/444-4080 or 246/444-2000; sandylane.com; doubles from $$$$$

BERMUDA

Cambridge Beaches Gracious resort of 94 cottages spread along 30 acres on the island's west end. 800/468-7300 or 441/234-0331; cambridge beaches.com; doubles from $$, including breakfast

BERMUDA

Elbow Beach Much-loved hotel with 50 acres of gardens and prime beachfront, in the process of being rebranded as a Mandarin Oriental. Renovations are ongoing. 800/526-6566 or 441/236-3535; mandarinoriental. com; doubles from $$

BERMUDA

The Reefs Cliffside property on the south shore of the island—recently reopened after major renovations. 800/742-2008 or 441/238-0222; thereefs.com; doubles from $$

BERMUDA

Waterloo House A 19th-century manor house with traditional English interiors on Hamilton Harbour. 800/468-4100 or 441/ 295-4480; waterloohouse. com; doubles from $$

CAYMAN ISLANDS

Ritz-Carlton, Grand Cayman Imposing 144-acre compound on a peninsula-like stretch of Seven Mile Beach. 800/241-3333 or 011-345/943-9000; ritzcarlton.com; doubles from $$$

DOMINICA

Jungle Bay Spa & Resort Eco-friendly cluster of cottages set on a lush mountainside. 767/446-1789; junglebaydominica. com; doubles from $$

DOMINICAN REPUBLIC

Puntacana Resort & Club Sprawling 15,000-acre complex including newly refurbished casitas and Tortuga Bay, a boutique property within the resort designed by Oscar de la Renta. 888/442-2262 or 809/959-2262; puntacana. com; doubles at Puntacana from $$; doubles at Tortuga Bay from $$$$

JAMAICA

Couples Negril A 234-room resort with colorful local touches on the island's western end. 800/268-7537 or 876/ 957-5960; couples. com; doubles from $$, all-inclusive

JAMAICA

Couples Sans Souci Contemporary 35-acre haven carved into the cliffs along the northern coast. 800/268-7537 or 876/994-1206; couples. com; doubles from $$$, all-inclusive

JAMAICA
Grand Lido Braco Resort & Spa Resort resembling a Caribbean village with a town square. 800/467-8737 or 876/954-0000; grandlido braco.com; doubles from $$, all-inclusive

JAMAICA
Jamaica Inn Ethereal cottages and a manor high on a 6-acre bluff above a white-sand shoreline. 800/837-4608 or 876/974-2515; jamaicainn.com; doubles from $$$

JAMAICA
Ritz-Carlton Golf & Spa Resort, Rose Hall Expansive resort with pastel-hued rooms on Montego Bay. 800/241-3333 or 876/953-2800; ritzcarlton.com; doubles from $$$

JAMAICA
Rockhouse Hotel Chic and eclectic boutique hotel with an eco-friendly ethos. 876/957-4373; rockhouse hotel.com; doubles from $

JAMAICA
Round Hill Hotel & Villas Storied former plantation on 110 acres fronting Montego Bay. 800/972-2159 or 876/956-7050; roundhill jamaica.com; doubles from $$$

JAMAICA
Royal Plantation, Ocho Rios Opulently decorated complex in a secluded cove. 888/487-6925 or 876/974-5601; royalplantation.com; doubles from $$$

NEVIS
Four Seasons Resort Colorful resort amid lush gardens along the calm waters of Pinney's Beach. 800/332-3442 or 869/469-1111; fourseasons.com; doubles from $$$$

PETER ISLAND
Peter Island Resort Private island with bungalows spread across 1,800 acres. 800/346-4451 or 284/495-2000; peterisland.com; doubles from $$$$, including meals

PUERTO RICO
Horned Dorset Primavera Spanish-colonial hideaway fresh from a complete renovation last year. 800/633-1857 or 787/823-4050; horned dorset.com; doubles from $$$$

ST. BART'S
Eden Rock Hotel Legendary hotel on a rocky promontory jutting into the Baie de St. Jean. 877/563-7105 or 590-590/297-999; eden rockhotel.com; doubles from $$$$, including breakfast

ST. BART'S
Hotel Guanahani & Spa Brightly colored West Indian bungalows between a white-sand beach and a lagoon. 800/216-3774 or 590-590/276-660; leguanahani.com; doubles from $$$$, including breakfast

ST. BART'S
Hotel Saint-Barth Isle de France Fashionable property on a quiet stretch of the Baie des Flamands. 800/810-4691 or 590-590/276-181; isle-de-france.com; doubles from $$$$$

ST. LUCIA
Discovery at Marigot Bay Classic resort reimagined with streamlined and modern flair. 758/458-5300; discoverystlucia.com; doubles from $$

ST. LUCIA
Jade Mountain Open-air suites with private infinity pools and views of the Pitons in a resort-within-a resort at Anse Chastenet. 800/223-1108 or 758/459-4000; jademountainstlucia.com; doubles from $$$$$

ST. LUCIA
Ladera Luxe lodge on a forested ridge 1,100 feet above the water. 866/290-0978 or 758/459-7323; ladera.com; doubles from $$, including breakfast

TURKS AND CAICOS
Grace Bay Club All-suite resort with sophisticated touches. 800/946-5757 or 649/946-5757; gracebay club.com; doubles from $$$$

TURKS AND CAICOS
Parrot Cay Trendsetting villas on a private 1,000-acre island. 877/754-0726 or 649/946-7788; parrotcay.como.bz; doubles from $$$$, including breakfast

VIRGIN GORDA
Biras Creek Collection of suites on a 140-acre peninsula framed by a white-sand beach and Berchers Bay. 800/223-1108 or 284/494-3555; biras.com; doubles from $$$$

VIRGIN GORDA
Rosewood Little Dix Bay 100 airy and recently updated shingled rooms on a secluded bay. 888/767-3966 or 284/495-5555; littledixbay.com; doubles from $$$

The arrival
dock at Antigua's
Jumby Bay.

Auchterarder

Ballantrae

Adare

Ballinakill   Newport   Builth Wells

Skenfrith

London

West Sussex

Amsterdam

Berlin

Reims

Paris

Pra

Onzain

Baden-
Baden

Munich

Zurich

Lausanne   Venice

Interlaken

Tamniès   Cernobbio

Laguiole   Milan   Asolo

St.-Paul de Vence   Vescovana

Martillac   Moustieres-Ste.-Marie   Taglio
di Po

Maussane les Alpilles   Mougins   Fiesole   Rimin

Avignon   Canale

Nîmes   Greve
Les Baux-   in Chianti   Cortona
de-Provence

Madrid   Cannes

Antibes   Porto
Èze   Ercole   Rome

Monte
Carlo

Positano

Majorca   Amalfi   Capri

Ravel

Taormina

Modica

Siracu

EUROPE

THE BLACK SEA

Vienna
Budapest

Tulcea

Sochi

Istanbul

Athens

Rhodes

Santorini

AUSTRIA

VIENNA

Vienna Hotel Imperial
Opulent 1863 palace, former home of the Prince of Württemberg, on the Ring near the Kärntnerstrasse. 16 Kärntner Ring; 800/325-3589 or 43-1/501-100; starwoodhotels.com; doubles from $$$$$

CZECH REPUBLIC

PRAGUE

Four Seasons Hotel
Complex of interconnected Baroque, Neoclassical, and Renaissance buildings, steps from the Charles Bridge. 2A/1098 Veleslavinova; 800/332-3442 or 420-2/2142-7000; fourseasons.com; doubles from $$

ENGLAND

LONDON

Dukes Hotel 1908 hotel in two freshly renovated Georgian town houses near Green Park. St. James's Place; 44-20/7491-4840; dukeshotel.com; doubles from $$$

LONDON

41 Discreet and clubby retreat with copious amounts of mahogany and black leather, opposite Buckingham Palace's Royal Mews. 41 Buckingham Palace Rd.; 44-20/

7300-0041; 41hotel.com; doubles from $$$

LONDON

Four Seasons Hotel
9-story Mayfair property with a quiet take on English style, just off Hyde Park. Hamilton Place, Park Lane; 800/332-3442 or 44-20/7499-0888; fourseasons.com; doubles from $$$$

LONDON

The Goring Classic family-run hotel dating from 1910, with secluded gardens, on a quiet Belgravia street. Beeston Place; 44-20/7396-9000; goringhotel.co.uk; doubles from $$$$

LONDON

InterContinental Park Lane Storied hotel in a stellar location between Knightsbridge and Mayfair; a $113 million makeover has just been completed. 1 Hamilton Place; 800/327-0200 or 44-20/7409-3131; intercontinental.com; doubles from $$

LONDON

Milestone Hotel
Stately red-brick Victorian hotel with antiques-filled interiors, opposite Kensington Palace. 1 Kensington Court; 800/223-6800 or

44-20/7917-1000; milestonehotel.com; doubles from $$$

LONDON

Sloane Square Recently revamped Chelsea property with pared-down British flair. Sloane Square; 44-20/7896-9988; sloanesquarehotel.co.uk; doubles from $$

WEST SUSSEX

Gravetye Manor
Elizabethan-era manor 90 minutes south of London. Near East Grinstead; 800/735-2478 or 44-1342/810-567; gravetyemanor.co.uk; doubles from $$

FRANCE

AVEYRON

Hotel-Restaurant Bras
Glass-walled hotel and adjacent Michelin 3-starred restaurant, in a pastoral setting. Laguiole; 800/735-2478 or 33-5/65-51-18-20; michel-bras.fr; doubles from $$

BORDEAUX

Les Sources de Caudalie
58-room hotel and spa set among vineyards, with grape-based beauty treatments and a hammam. Martillac; 33-5/57-83-83-83; sources-caudalie.com; doubles from $$$

CÔTE D'AZUR

Château de la Chèvre d'Or Clifftop complex of charming stone buildings overlooking a medieval village. Èze; 800/735-2478 or 33-4/92-10-66-66; chevredor.com; doubles from $$

CÔTE D'AZUR

La Colombe d'Or Family-run villa at the entrance to a fortified village, 12 miles from Nice. St.-Paul de Vence; 33-4/93-32-80-02; la-colombe-dor.com; doubles from $$

CÔTE D'AZUR

Hôtel du Cap Eden Roc
19th-century mansion surrounded by 22 acres of gardens on the tip of a peninsula. Antibes; 33-4/93-61-39-01; edenroc-hotel.fr; doubles from $$$$

CÔTE D'AZUR

InterContinental Carlton Cannes Palatial 1912 hotel on La Croisette, the historic waterfront promenade. Cannes; 888/424-6835 or 33-4/93-06-40-06; intercontinental.com; doubles from $$$

CÔTE D'AZUR

Le Manoir de l'Etang
Ivy-covered villa with a pool

The restaurant at
Caol Ishka, in Sicily.

and a lotus flower–filled lake 5 miles from Cannes. Mougins; 33-4/92-28-36-00; manoir-de-letang.com; doubles from $$

DORDOGNE
Le Canard a Trois Pattes Limestone farmhouse dating from the 15th century, with design-centric contemporary interiors. Le Castanet, Tamniès; 33-5/53-59-13-85; troispattes.com; doubles from $

LOIRE VALLEY
Domaine des Hauts de Loire 19th-century former hunting lodge in a 178-acre wooded park. Onzain; 800/735-2478 or 33-2/54-20-72-57; domainehautsloire.com; doubles from $$, including breakfast

NÎMES
Jardins Secrets Romantic downtown retreat with a swimming pool surrounded by orange and olive trees. 3 Rue Gaston Maruejols; 33-4/66-84-82-64; jardins secrets.net; doubles from $$

PARIS
Five Hotel Modern Latin Quarter boutique hotel near the shopping street of Rue Mouffetard. 3 Rue Flatters;

33-1/43-31-74-21; thefive hotel.com; doubles from $

PARIS
Four Seasons Hotel George V Majestic 1928 white-stone hotel with standard-setting service and a Michelin 2-starred restaurant. 31 Ave. George V; 800/332-3442 or 33-1/ 49-52-70-00; fourseasons. com; doubles from $$$$$

PARIS
Hôtel Fouquet's Barrière Sleek 107-room palace hotel on the Champs-Élysées with Jacques Garcia–designed interiors. 46 Ave. George V; 800/223-6800 or 33-1/40-69-60-00; fouquets-barriere.com; doubles from $$$$$

PARIS
Hôtel Plaza Athénée Discreet 1911 hotel in the midst of the city's most exclusive designer boutiques. 25 Ave. Montaigne; 800/223-6800 or 33-1/53-67-66-65; plaza-athenee-paris.com; doubles from $$$$$

PARIS
Le Meurice Louis XVI–style hotel across from the Tuileries, between the Place de la Concorde and the Louvre. 228 Rue de

Rivoli; 800/650-1842 or 33-1/44-58-10-10; meuricehotel.com; doubles from $$$$$

PARIS
The Ritz Iconic 1898 palace on the city's most famous square. 15 Place Vendôme; 800/223-6800 or 33-1/43-16-30-30; ritzparis. com; doubles from $$$$$

PROVENCE
Hôtel d'Europe 16th-century mansion that has hosted Victor Hugo and Jackie O., just inside the town walls. Avignon; 33-4/90-14-76-76; heurope.com; doubles from $

PROVENCE
La Bastide de Moustiers Chef Alain Ducasse's intimate inn on 10 acres in the craggy southern Alps of Haute-Provence. Moustiers-Ste.-Marie; 33-4/92-70-47-47; bastide-moustiers.com; doubles from $$

PROVENCE
L'Ange et l'Elephant An eclectically decorated guesthouse with a restaurant and tea salon, a short walk from town. Maussane les Alpilles; 33-4/90-54-18-34; elephange.com; doubles from $

PROVENCE
L'Oustau de Baumanière Three historic buildings, once favored by Winston Churchill and Elizabeth Taylor, at the edge of a picturesque village. Les Baux-de-Provence; 800/735-2478 or 33-4/90-54-33-07; oustaudebaumaniere.com; doubles from $$

REIMS
Château Les Crayères Stately château on a private 17-acre park a few minutes from town. 800/735-2478 or 33-3/26-82-80-80; lescrayeres.com; doubles from $$

GERMANY
BADEN-BADEN
Brenner's Park-Hotel & Spa Legendary 19th-century resort near the Black Forest. 4–6 Schillerstrasse; 800/628-8929 or 49-7/221-9000; brenners.com; doubles from $$$

BERLIN
Hotel de Rome Grand new hotel in the former headquarters of the Dresdner Bank. 37 Behrenstrasse; 888/ 667-9477 or 49-30/ 460-6090; hotelderome. com; doubles from $$

BERLIN
Ritz-Carlton An 11-story Art Deco tower beside Tiergarten park. 3 Potsdamer Platz; 800/241-3333 or 49-30/337-777; ritzcarlton.com; doubles from $$

BERLIN
Sofitel Berlin Gendarmenmarkt Central hotel with views of the French Cathedral. 50–52 Charlottenstrasse; 800/763-4835 or 49-30/203-750; sofitel.com; doubles from $$

MUNICH
Mandarin Oriental Neo-Renaissance building next to Maximilianstrasse. 1 Neuturmstrasse; 800/526-6566 or 49-89/290-980; mandarinoriental.com; doubles from $$$

GREECE
ATHENS
O & B Boutique Hotel 11-room contemporary hotel with a lively lobby scene, walking distance from the Parthenon. 7 Leokoriou St.; 30-210/331-2950; oandbhotel. com; doubles from $$

RHODES
Melenos Lindos White-washed buildings with local touches, overlooking a stunning harbor. 30-22/4403-2222; melenoslindos. com; doubles from $$$

SANTORINI
Katikies Hotel Aegean-style buildings on a cliff above the caldera. 30-228/607-1401; katikies. com; doubles from $$$, including breakfast

HUNGARY
BUDAPEST
Four Seasons Hotel Gresham Palace Art Nouveau building with Danube views. 5–6 Roosevelt Tér; 800/332-3442 or 36-1/411-9000; fourseasons.com; doubles from $$

IRELAND
CO. LIMERICK
Adare Manor Hotel & Golf Resort Tudor-Revival castle with a golf course. Adare; 800/462-3273 or 353-61/396-566; adaremanor.com; doubles from $$$

CO. WATERFORD
Waterford Castle Hotel & Golf Club 17th-century castle on an island in the River Suir. Ballinakill; 353-51/878-203; waterfordcastle. com; doubles from $$

ITALY
AMALFI COAST
Hotel Santa Caterina Mountaintop Belle Époque villas with a newly completed all-suite wing. Amalfi; 800/223-6800 or 39-089/871-012; hotelsanta caterina.it; doubles from $$, including breakfast

AMALFI COAST
Il San Pietro di Positano Stunning family-owned property carved into the Lattari Mountains. Positano; 39-089/875-455; ilsanpietro. it; doubles from $$$

AMALFI COAST
La Rosa dei Venti Cliffside inn with painted-wood furniture and colorful ceramic-tiled floors near Fornillo beach. Positano; 39-089/875-252; larosa deiventi.com doubles from $, including breakfast

AMALFI COAST
Le Sirenuse Glamorous 18th-century villa with whitewashed walls, over-looking the sea. Positano; 800/223-6800 or 39-089/875-066; sirenuse.it; doubles from $$$, including breakfast

AMALFI COAST
Palazzo Sasso Regal 12th-century pink villa set high above the Mediter-ranean. Ravello; 39-089/818-181; palazzosasso. com; doubles from $$$, including breakfast

CAPRI
Capri Palace Hotel & Spa Art-filled Mediterranean hotel and wellness sanctuary in Anacapri. 39-081/978-0111; capri palace.com; doubles from $$$, including breakfast

CAPRI
Grand Hotel Quisisana 19th-century icon with a decidedly old-world feel, near the island's famous Faraglioni rocks. 800/223-6800 or 39-081/837-0788; quisi.it; doubles from $$$, including breakfast

CORTONA
Il Falconiere Cluster of rustic 17th-century buildings on a wine estate, close to Tuscany and Umbria. 800/735-2478 or 39-05/7561-2679; ilfalconiere.it; doubles from $$, including breakfast

FLORENCE AREA
Villa San Michele Former 15th-century monastery in the hills above Florence, with a Michelangelo-credited façade. Fiesole; 800/237-1236 or 39-055/567-8200; villasanmichele. com; doubles from $$$$$, including breakfast

LAKE COMO
Villa d'Este Prestigious lakeside property on 25

The Inn at the
Roman Forum,
in Rome.

acres. Cernobbio; 800/ 223-6800 or 39-031/3481; villadeste.it; doubles from $$$$

MILAN

Nhow Former factory with a revolving showcase of contemporary art, in the bustling Tortona district. 35 Via Tortona; 39-02/ 489-8861; nhow-hotels. com; doubles from $$$$

MILAN

Vietnamonamour 1903 villa with a Southeast Asian aesthetic in the residential enclave of Città Studi. 7 Via A. Pestalozza; 39-02/7063- 4614; vietnamonamour.com; doubles from $, including breakfast

PIEDMONT

Villa Tiboldi 9-room villa set amid vineyards; the popular restaurant serves regional food. Canale; 39-0173/970-388; villa tiboldi.it; doubles from $

PORTO ERCOLE

Il Pellicano Romantic clifftop hideaway with a seawater pool. 39-0564/ 858-111; pellicanohotel. com; doubles from $$$$, including breakfast

RIMINI

Duomo Hotel New Ron Arad-designed hotel

with futuristic interiors in a seaside town. 28 Via G. Bruno; 39-0541/24215; duomohotel.com; doubles from $$

ROME

Hotel Hassler Turn-of- the-century palace above the Spanish Steps. 6 Piazza Trinità dei Monti; 800/223- 6800 or 39-06/699-340; hotelhasslerroma.com; doubles from $$$$$

ROME

Inn at the Roman Forum Posh, intimate hotel with a rooftop garden, in the heart of town. 30 Via degli Ibernesi; 39-06/6919-0970; theinnattheromanforum. com; doubles from $$$, including breakfast

ROME

Portrait Suites Chic 14-room palazzo owned by the Ferragamo family, a short stroll from the Spanish Steps. 23 Via Bocca di Leone; 39-06/ 6938-0742; lungarnohotels. com; doubles from $$$, including breakfast

ROME

St. Regis Grand Hotel Opulent 19th-century palace designed by César Ritz, a 5-minute walk from the Via Veneto. 3 Via Vittorio E. Orlando; 800/

325-3589 or 39-06/47091; starwoodhotels.com; doubles from $$$

ROME

Villa Spalletti Trivelli Former count's residence near the Trevi Fountain, fresh from a $7 million redo. 4 Via Piacenza; 39-06/ 4890-7934; villaspalletti.it; doubles from $$$$$

ROME

Westin Excelsior Grand- dame hotel three blocks from the Villa Borghese gardens. 125 Via Vittorio Veneto; 800/325-3589 or 39-06/47081; westin.com; doubles from $$$$

SICILY

Caol Ishka Hotel Historic farm on the Anapo River, converted into a stylish retreat. Siracusa; 39-0931/ 69057; caolishka.com; doubles from $$

SICILY

Casa Talia B&B of five stone houses with contemporary interiors, on a ridge overlooking a village. Modica; 39-0932/ 752-075; casatalia.com; doubles from $, including breakfast

SICILY

Grand Hotel Timeo 19th-century hotel complex

next to the Greek Theater and facing Mount Etna. Taormina; 39-0942/23801; framonhotelgroup.com; doubles from $$$, including breakfast

TUSCANY

Villa Bordoni Restored 16th-century Tuscan manor with gardens. Greve in Chianti; 39-055/884-0004; villabordoni.it; doubles from $$, including breakfast

VENETO

Ca'Zen Historic hunting lodge on the banks of the Po River. Taglio di Po; 39- 0426/346-469; tenutacazen. it; doubles from $, including breakfast

VENETO

Hotel Villa Cipriani Peaceful 16th-century villa in a hillside village an hour from Venice. Asolo; 800/ 325-3535 or 39-0423/523- 411; starwoodhotels.com; doubles from $$$

VENETO

Villa Pisani Sprawling estate with Veronese frescoes and celebrated gardens. Vescovana; 39-0425/920-016; villa pisani.it; doubles from $

VENICE

Bauer Il Palazzo 18th-century property

with a Gothic-Byzantine façade on the Grand Canal. 1413/D San Marco; 800/223-6800 or 39-041/520-7022; ilpalazzovenezia.it; doubles from $$$$$

VENICE

San Clemente Palace & Resort Former monastery on the private 17-acre San Clemente Island. 1 Isola di San Clemente; 800/223-6800 or 39-041/244-5001; sanclemente.thi.it; doubles from $$$$, including breakfast

MONACO

MONTE CARLO

Hôtel Hermitage Fin-de-siècle palace on a cliff above the harbor. Square Beaumarchais; 800/223-6800 or 377/98-06-40-00; montecarloresort. com; doubles from $$$

THE NETHERLANDS

AMSTERDAM

The Dylan Opulent hotel designed by Anouska Hempel on Keizersgracht canal. 384 Keizersgracht; 31-20/530-2010; dylan amsterdam.com; doubles from $$$

ROMANIA

TULCEA

Delta Nature Resort Timber villas on the shore of Lake Somova, in ancient forest.

40-21/311-4532; delta resort.com; doubles from $$, including breakfast

RUSSIA

SOCHI

Grand Hotel Rodina Refurbished Stalin-era villa in a Black Sea resort town. 33 Vinogradnaya St.; 7-8622/539-000; grand hotelrodina.ru; doubles from $$$

SCOTLAND

BALLANTRAE

Glenapp Castle Romantic 19th-century manor overlooking the Irish Sea. 800/735-2478 or 44-1465/831-212; glenapp castle.com; doubles from $$$$, including breakfast and dinner

PERTHSHIRE

Gleneagles 1924 golf retreat in the hills; a spa is scheduled to open this spring. Auchterarder; 866/463-8734 or 44-1764/662-231; gleneagles.com; doubles from $$$$, including breakfast

SPAIN

MADRID

Room Mate Alicia Intimately scaled outpost with colorful rooms on the Plaza de Santa Ana. 2 Calle Prado; 34/91-389-6095; roommate hotels.com; doubles from $

MAJORCA

Palacio Ca Sa Galesa Historic 16th-century manor tucked behind the cathedral in Palma's Gothic district. 34/971-715-400; palaciocasagalesa.com; doubles from $$

SWITZERLAND

INTERLAKEN

Victoria-Jungfrau Grand Hotel & Spa Belle Époque resort, a society favorite since 1865, in the Bernese Oberland. 800/223-6800 or 41-33/828-2828; victoria jungfrau.ch; doubles from $$$$

LAUSANNE

Beau-Rivage Palace Historic hotel on 10 manicured acres beside Lake Geneva. 17–19 Place du Port; 800/223-6800 or 41-21/613-3333; brp.ch; doubles from $$

ZURICH

Baur au Lac Family-owned 1844 hotel with lake views in Zurich's fashionable center. 1 Talstrasse; 800/223-6800 or 41-44/220-5020; bauraulac.ch; doubles from $$$

TURKEY

ISTANBUL

Four Seasons Hotel at Sultanahmet Neoclassical building with Turkish-

inspired interiors near the Hagia Sophia. 1 Tevkifhane Sokak; 800/332-3442 or 90-212/ 638-8200; fourseasons. com; doubles from $$$

ISTANBUL

Ritz-Carlton Steel-and-glass tower with traditional décor, near the Bosporus. Suzer Plaza, 15 Elmadag Askerocagi Caddesi; 800/241-3333 or 90-212/334-4444; ritzcarlton.com; doubles from $$$

WALES

BUILTH WELLS

Drawing Room 3-room inn with a restaurant featuring local ingredients. 44-198/255-2493; the-drawing-room.co.uk; doubles from $$, including breakfast and dinner

PEMBROKESHIRE

Llys Meddyg Converted Georgian carriage house in the quiet coastal town of Newport. 44-1239/820-008; llysmeddyg.com; doubles from $, including breakfast

SKENFRITH

Bell at Skenfrith Former 17th-century coaching inn, recently renovated, set in the Monmouthshire countryside. 44-160/075-0235; skenfrith.co.uk; doubles from $, including breakfast

The reception area at Madrid's Room Mate Alicia.

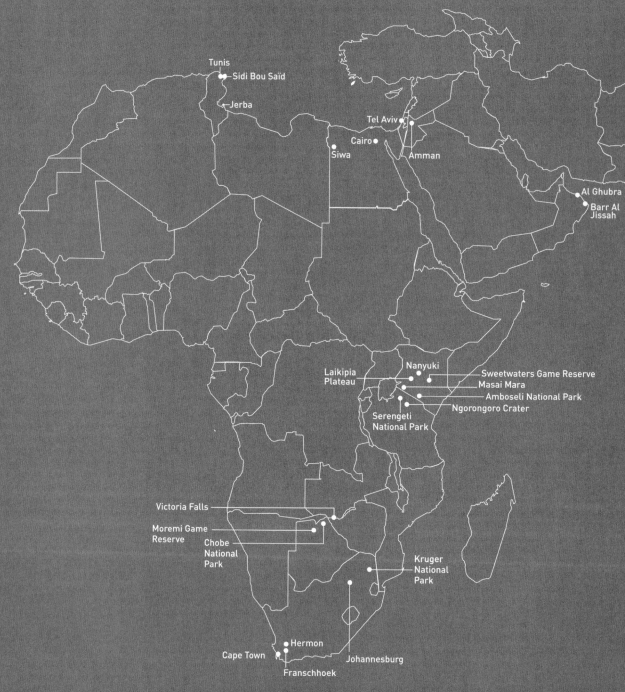

252

Tunis
Sidi Bou Saïd
Jerba

Tel Aviv
Cairo
Siwa
Amman

Al Ghubra
Barr Al Jissah

Nanyuki
Laikipia Plateau
Sweetwaters Game Reserve
Masai Mara
Amboseli National Park
Ngorongoro Crater
Serengeti National Park

Victoria Falls
Moremi Game Reserve
Chobe National Park

Kruger National Park

Hermon
Cape Town
Johannesburg
Franschhoek

AFRICA +
THE MIDDLE EAST

BOTSWANA

CHOBE NATIONAL PARK

Chobe Chilwero Lodge
Thatched cottages built
to resemble a village,
overlooking the Chobe
River. 800/554-7094
or 27-11/438-4650;
sanctuarylodges.com;
doubles from $$$$$,
including meals, drinks,
and activities

MOREMI GAME RESERVE

Jao Camp Chic safari
camp with Indonesian
touches, in the floodplains
of the Okavango Delta.
800/545-1910 or 27-11/
807-1800; wilderness-
safaris.com; doubles from
$$$$$, all-inclusive

MOREMI GAME RESERVE

Mombo Camp Intimate
camp of palatial 3-room
tents. 800/545-1910 or
27-11/807-1800; wilderness-
safaris.com; doubles from
$$$$$, including meals,
drinks, and activities

EGYPT

CAIRO

**Four Seasons Hotel at the
First Residence** Resplen-
dent Neoclassical-style
tower with views of the
Pyramids and the Nile.
35 Giza St.; 800/332-3442
or 20-2/3573-1212; four
seasons.com; doubles
from $$

CAIRO

**Four Seasons Hotel
at Nile Plaza** 30-story
property just beyond
Garden City. 1089 Corniche
El Nil; 800/332-3442
or 20-2/2791-5000; four
seasons.com; doubles
from $$

SIWA

Adrère Amellal Oasis
Berber-style fortress
on the Siwa oasis, an
8-hour drive from Cairo.
20-2/2736-7879; adrere
amellal.net; doubles
from $$, including meals
and activities

ISRAEL

TEL AVIV

Nina Café Suites Hotel
Art Deco–inspired hotel
in the bohemian Neve
Tzedek district. 29 Shabazi
St.; 972-52/508-4141;
ninacafehotel.com;
doubles from $$,
including breakfast

JORDAN

AMMAN

Four Seasons Hotel
15-story hotel between
the Al Sweifiyah resi-
dential area and the
financial district. 5th
Circle, Al-Kindi St.,
Jabal Amman; 800/332-
3442 or 962-6/550-
5555; fourseasons.
com; doubles from $$

KENYA

AMBOSELI NATIONAL PARK

**Amboseli Serena Safari
Lodge** Retreat inspired by
traditional Masai architec-
ture, in an acacia grove.
254-20/271-0511; serena
hotels.com; doubles from
$$, including meals

AMBOSELI NATIONAL PARK

Tortilis Camp Cluster of
intimate, eco-friendly tents
facing Mount Kilimanjaro.
254-20/603-091; tortilis.
com; doubles from $$$$,
including meals, drinks,
and activities

LAIKIPIA PLATEAU

Sanctuary at Ol Lentille
Four exquisite villas
within a 6,500-acre
conservancy on the
Laikipia Plateau, with
views of Mount Kenya.
888/588-4590; ol-lentille.
com; houses from $$$$$

MASAI MARA

**Fairmont Mara Safari
Club** Series of permanent
tents on the oxbow of
the Mara River. 800/441-
1414 or 254-20/216-940;
fairmont.com; doubles
from $$$, including meals,
drinks, and activities

MASAI MARA

Kichwa Tembo Pair of
1920's-style tented camps
overlooking the Mara

Plains. 888/882-3742 or
27-11/809-4300; ccafrica.
com; doubles from $$$$,
including meals, drinks,
and activities

NANYUKI

**Fairmont Mount Kenya
Safari Club** 1950's-era
hunting lodge favored
by the Hollywood elite.
800/441-1414 or 254-
20/216-940; fairmont.
com; doubles from $$,
including meals, drinks,
and activities

**SWEETWATERS GAME
RESERVE**

Sweetwaters Tented Camp
Collection of thatched-roof
tents on a 90,000-acre
private reserve, with Mount
Kenya views. 254-20/
271-0511; serenahotels.
com; doubles from $$

OMAN

AL GHUBRA

Chedi Muscat A shimmer-
ing modern palace on
the Gulf of Oman.
968/2452-4400; chedi
muscat.com; doubles
from $$

BARR AL JISSAH

**Shangri-La Barr Al
Jissah** A 3-hotel complex
overlooking Al Jissah
Bay, just south of Muscat.
968/2477-6666; shangri-la.
com; doubles from $$

SOUTH AFRICA

CAPE TOWN

Cape Grace Classic hotel with modern touches on the water. W. Quay Rd., Victoria & Alfred Waterfront; 800/223-6800 or 27-21/410-7100; capegrace.com; doubles from $$$, including breakfast

CAPE TOWN

Mount Nelson Hotel Stately 1899 hotel on 9 acres at the foot of Table Mountain. 76 Orange St.; 800/237-1236 or 27-21/483-1000; mount nelson.co.za; doubles from $$$$, including breakfast

CAPE TOWN

Table Bay Hotel Victorian-style property on a seaside promenade. Quay 6, Victoria & Alfred Waterfront; 800/223-6800 or 27-21/406-5000; suninternational.com; doubles from $$$

FRANSCHHOEK

Le Quartier Français Tranquil inn with one of South Africa's top restaurants, in the heart of a charming historic village. 27-21/876-2151; lequartier.co.za; doubles from $$, including breakfast

JOHANNESBURG

Clico Guest House Chic B&B with a Cape Dutch façade in Rosebank. 27 Sturdee Ave.; 27-11/252-3300; clicoguesthouse.com; doubles from $, including breakfast

JOHANNESBURG

Westcliff Hotel Tuscan-style hotel on a ridge above the city. 800/237-1236 or 27-11/481-6000; westcliff.co.za; doubles from $$$

KRUGER NATIONAL PARK AREA

Londolozi Legendary camps and suites in a private game reserve. 800/735-2478 or 27-11/280-6640; londolozi.com; doubles from $$$$$, including meals, drinks, and activities

KRUGER NATIONAL PARK AREA

MalaMala Game Reserve Trio of renowned bush camps on 33,000 acres along the Sand River. 27-11/442-2267; malamala.com; doubles from $$$$$, including meals and activities

KRUGER NATIONAL PARK AREA

Sabi Sabi Private Game Reserve Four lodges ranging in style from colonial to eco-futuristic. 27-11/447-7172; sabisabi.com; doubles from $$$$, including meals, drinks, and activities

KRUGER NATIONAL PARK AREA

Singita Sabi Sand Four exceptionally well-designed lodges in the African bush. 27-21/683-3424; singita.com; doubles from $$$$$, including meals, drinks, and activities

HERMON

Bartholomeus Klip Farmhouse A 17,000-acre farm and game reserve in the Swartland wine region, about 60 miles from Cape Town. 27-22/448-1820; bartholomeus klip.com; doubles from $$$, all-inclusive

TANZANIA

NGORONGORO CRATER

Ngorongoro Crater Lodge Spectacularly designed huts on stilts, along the rim of the world's largest crater. 888/882-3742 or 27-11/809-4300; ccafrica.com; doubles from $$$$$, including meals, drinks, and activities

NGORONGORO CRATER

Ngorongoro Serena Safari Lodge Eco-minded lodge with prehistoric motifs on the walls and Masai carvings. 254-20/271-0511; serena hotels.com; doubles from $$$, including meals

SERENGETI NATIONAL PARK

Kirawira Camp Edwardian-style tented camp in the Western Serengeti. 800/525-4800 or 254-20/271-0511; serenahotels.com; doubles from $$$$$, including meals, drinks, and game drives

TUNISIA

JERBA

Dar Dhiafa A rusticchic retreat in a village on the island of Jerba. 216-75/671-166; hoteldardhiafa.com; doubles from $

SIDI BOU SAÏD

Dar Saïd 19-century town house with lush gardens, in a hilltop village overlooking the Gulf of Tunis. 216-71/729-666; darsaid.com.tn; doubles from $

TUNIS

Dar el Medina A converted family mansion steps from the casbah. 64 Rue Sidi Ben Arous, La Medina; 216-71/563-022; darel medina.com; doubles from $, including breakfast

ZAMBIA

VICTORIA FALLS

Royal Livingstone Graceful property with colonial-style buildings on the banks of the Zambezi River. 260-213/321-122; suninternational.com; doubles from $$$$

Ngorongoro Crater
Lodge, in Tanzania.

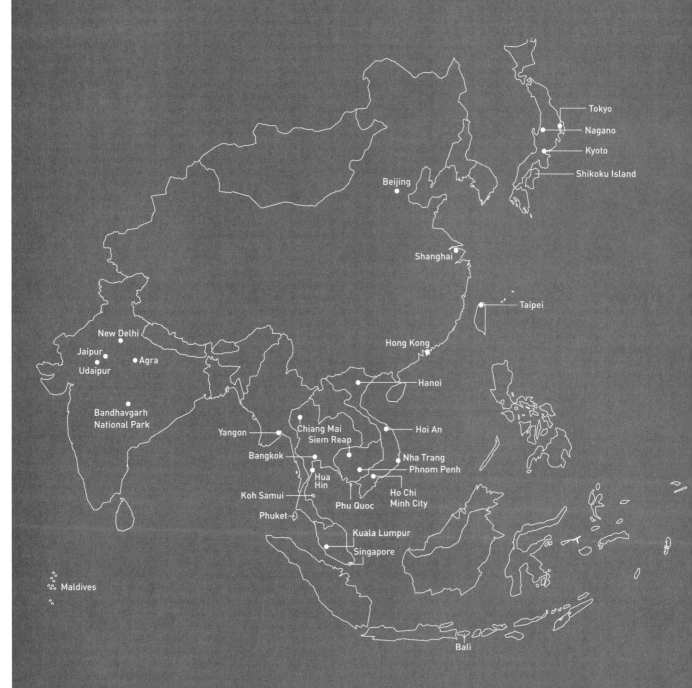

Tokyo
Nagano
Kyoto
Shikoku Island

Beijing

Shanghai

Taipei

New Delhi
Jaipur
Udaipur
Agra

Hong Kong

Hanoi

Bandhavgarh
National Park

Yangon

Chiang Mai
Siem Reap

Hoi An

Bangkok

Nha Trang
Phnom Penh

Hua
Hin

Koh Samui

Phu Quoc

Ho Chi
Minh City

Phuket

Kuala Lumpur

Singapore

Maldives

Bali

ASIA

CAMBODIA

PHNOM PENH

Raffles Hotel Le Royal
1929 French-colonial mansion in the city center. 92 Rukhak Vithei Daun Penh; 800/768-9009 or 855-23/981-888; raffles. com; doubles from $$, including breakfast

SIEM REAP

Raffles Grand Hotel d'Angkor Updated classic hotel in the heart of Siem Reap. 800/768-9009 or 855-63/963-888; raffles. com; doubles from $$, including breakfast

CHINA

BEIJING

Peninsula Beijing This opulent property, with Chinese interiors, has undergone a $35 million refurbishment. 8 Goldfish Lane; 866/382-8388 or 86-10/8516-2888; peninsula.com; doubles from $$, including breakfast

BEIJING

St. Regis Hotel Sleek high-rise in the middle of the Jian Guo Men Wai business district and shopping area. Currently closed for renovations and scheduled to reopen in May. Jian Guo Men Wai Rd.; 877/787-3447 or 86-10/6460-6688; stregis. com; doubles from $$$

HONG KONG

Four Seasons Hotel
Modern hotel located in the International Finance Center on Hong Kong Island, steps from the Star Ferry. 8 Finance St.; 800/332-3442 or 852/3196-8888; four seasons.com; doubles from $$$

HONG KONG

Grand Hyatt Palace hotel with a soaring lobby and ethereal rooms centrally located on Hong Kong Island. 1 Harbour Rd.; 800/233-1234 or 852/2588-1234; hyatt.com; doubles from $$

HONG KONG

The InterContinental
Contemporary 17-story hotel with spectacular views, on the Kowloon waterfront. 18 Salisbury Rd.; 800/327-0200 or 852/2721-1211; intercontinental. com; doubles from $$$

HONG KONG

Island Shangri-La
European and Asian touches in a skyscraper atop the Pacific Place mall, in the financial district. Supreme Court Rd.; 866/565-5050 or 852/2877-3838; shangri-la.com; doubles from $$$

HONG KONG

Kowloon Shangri-La
A grand waterfront fixture with a stunning 2-story lobby in Kowloon's Tsim Sha Tsui East. 64 Mody Rd.; 866/565-5050 or 852/2721-2111; shangri-la. com; doubles from $$

HONG KONG

Langham Hotel European-style hotel blocks from the harbor. 8 Peking Rd.; 800/588-9141 or 852/3552-3388; langhamhotels.com; doubles from $$

HONG KONG

Mandarin Oriental A storied 45-year-old institution in the business district, recently reopened after a $140 million overhaul. 5 Connaught Rd.; 800/526-6566 or 852/2522-0111; mandarinoriental.com; doubles from $$$

HONG KONG

Peninsula Hong Kong
Grand 1928 hotel on Victoria Harbour, minutes from museums and the MTR. Salisbury Rd.; 866/382-8388 or 852/2920-2888; peninsula.com; doubles from $$

SHANGHAI

Four Seasons Hotel
Well-rounded hotel with residential-style rooms near People's Square. 500 Weihai Rd.; 800/332-3442 or 86-21/6256-8888; fourseasons.com; doubles from $$

SHANGHAI

JW Marriott Hotel at Tomorrow Square
Streamlined rooms in the top floors of a 60-story complex close to the Bund. 399 Nanjing West Rd.; 800/228-9290 or 86-21/5359-4969; marriotthotels. com; doubles from $$

SHANGHAI

Pudong Shangri-La
Two towers on the eastern bank of the Huangpu River. 33 Fu Cheng Rd.; 866/565-5050 or 86-21/6882-8888; shangri-la.com; doubles from $$

SHANGHAI

The Regent Colorful and contemporary high-rise hotel. 1116 Yan An West Rd.; 888/201-1806 or 86-21/6115-9988; regenthotels. com; doubles from $$

SHANGHAI

St. Regis Hotel
328 rooms blend traditional and Asian elements in the Pudong district. 889 Dong Fang Rd.; 877/787-3447 or 86-21/5050-4567; stregis.com; doubles from $$

SHANGHAI
Westin Bund Center
Sleek property with an impressive art collection 5 minutes from the waterfront. 88 Henan Central Rd.; 800/228-3000 or 86-21/6335-1888; westin.com; doubles from $$

INDIA

AGRA
Oberoi Amarvilas Contemporary Moorish and Moghul fantasy of marble pools and fountains in the shadow of the Taj Mahal. 800/562-3764 or 91-562/223-1515; oberoiamarvilas.com; doubles from $$$$

JAIPUR
Oberoi Rajvilas Rajasthani fortress with luxury tents and villas, on the edge of the fabled pink city of Jaipur. 800/562-3764 or 91-141/268-0101; oberoi rajvilas.com; doubles from $$$$

MADHYA PRADESH
Mahua Kothi Complex of cottages modeled after traditional jungle dwellings on 40 acres near Bandhavgarh National Park. 866/969-1825; ccafrica.com; from $$$$ per person

NEW DELHI
The Imperial Ornate Victorian–meets–Art Deco landmark in the heart of town. Janpath; 800/323-7500 or 91-11/2334-1234; theimperialindia.com; doubles from $$$

UDAIPUR
Oberoi Udaivilas Impeccable palace in marble, sandstone, and gold leaf, set on 30 lakeside acres of former royal hunting grounds. 800/562-3764 or 91-294/243-3300; oberoi udaivilas.com; doubles from $$$

UDAIPUR
Taj Lake Palace Fairy-tale former royal residence rising from its own island in the middle of Lake Pichola. 866/969-1425 or 91-294/242-8800; tajhotels.com; doubles from $$$$

INDONESIA

BALI
Four Seasons Resort Bali at Jimbaran Bay Hillside villas with private plunge pools and outdoor lounge areas overlooking the beach. Guest rooms are currently being renovated, to be completed in April. 800/332-3442 or 62-361/701-010; fourseasons.com; doubles from $$$

BALI
Ritz-Carlton Bali Resort & Spa Set of stone cottages around a dramatic tiered infinity pool above the beach, on the southern tip of Jimbaran. 800/241-3333 or 62-361/702-222; ritzcarlton.com; doubles from $$

JAPAN

KYOTO
Yoshi-ima A 19th-century *ryokan* in the Gion district with traditional minimal interiors. Shinmonzen, Gion; 81-75/561-2620; yoshi-ima.co.jp; from $ per person, including meals

NAGANO
Oyado Kinenkan Spare, centuries-old inn famed for elaborate service, set in the Japanese alps. 550 Nishi-machi; 81-26/234-2043; from $ per person, including meals

SHIKOKU ISLAND
Utoco Deep Sea Therapy Center & Hotel Clean-lined spa complex perched near the Pacific. 81-8/8722-1811; utocods.co.jp; doubles from $$, including breakfast

TOKYO
Four Seasons Hotel at Chinzan-so Contemporary building surrounded by a historic garden, on the edge of Tokyo's business district. 10-8 Sekiguchi 2-chome, Bunkyo-ku; 800/332-3442 or 81-3/3943-2222; fourseasons.com; doubles from $$

TOKYO
Grand Hyatt Modernist mainstay in the Roppongi Hills food, art, and shopping complex. 6-10-3 Roppongi, Minato-ku; 800/233-1234 or 81-3/4333-1234; hyatt.com; doubles from $$$

TOKYO
Mandarin Oriental 179 serene rooms and a distinguished spa atop a Cesar Pelli–designed high-rise. 2-1-1 Nihonbashi Muromachi, Chuo-ku; 800/526-6566 or 81-3/3270-8950; mandarin oriental.com; doubles from $$$

TOKYO
Park Hyatt A classic fixture in the Shinjuku district—a hub for nightlife and shopping. 3-7-1-2 Nishi-Shinjuku, Shinjuku-ku; 800/223-1234 or 81-3/5322-1234; hyatt.com; doubles from $$$

TOKYO
Peninsula Tokyo 314-room hotel close to the Ginza, featuring Japanese design and tech-savvy touches. 1-8-1 Yurakucho, Chiyoda-ku; 866/382-8388 or 81-3/6270-2288; peninsula.com; doubles from $$$

The dining room at Mahua Kothi, in India.

TOKYO

Ritz-Carlton Traditional luxury in the bottom 3 and top 9 floors of the city's tallest tower, part of the new Tokyo Midtown complex. 9-7-1 Akasaka, Minato-ku; 800/241-3333 or 81-3/3423-8000; ritzcarlton.com; doubles from $$$

MALAYSIA

KUALA LUMPUR

Mandarin Oriental Locally-inflected 30-story hotel adjacent to the 88-story Petronas Twin Towers. Kuala Lumpur City Centre; 800/526-6566 or 60-3/2380-8888; mandarinoriental.com; doubles from $$

MALDIVES

FESDU ISLAND

W Retreat & Spa Maldives Design-centric villas on a private island west of Male. 877/946-8357 or 011-960/666-2222; whotels.com; doubles from $$$$$

MYANMAR

YANGON

The Strand 1901 landmark with exquisite details (Victorian colonnaded entry, inlaid teak, rattan furniture), in the city's commercial district. 92 Strand Rd.; 949/487-0522 or 951/243-377; ghmhotels.com; doubles from $$$, including breakfast

SINGAPORE

SINGAPORE

Fairmont Singapore Sophisticated outpost of sharply tailored guest rooms close to War Memorial Park. 80 Bras Basah Rd.; 800/441-1414 or 65/6339-7777; fairmont.com; doubles from $$

SINGAPORE

Four Seasons Hotel 20-story building with richly furnished rooms in the city's shopping and entertainment hub. 190 Orchard Blvd.; 800/332-3442 or 65/6734-1110; fourseasons.com; doubles from $$

SINGAPORE

The Fullerton Marble-filled contemporary hotel in the former general post office. 1 Fullerton Square; 800/323-7500 or 65/6733-8388; fullertonhotel.com; doubles from $$$

SINGAPORE

Raffles Hotel Gracious 19th-century classic with a tropical courtyard, in the business district. 1 Beach Rd.; 800/768-9009 or 65/6337-1886; raffles.com; doubles from $$$

SINGAPORE

Ritz-Carlton Millenia A 32-story building with a broad collection of contemporary art and a 7-acre garden, in the Marina Bay district. 7 Raffles Ave.; 800/241-3333 or 65/6337-8888; ritzcarlton.com; doubles from $$

TAIWAN

TAIPEI

Shangri-La's Far Eastern Plaza Hotel Rooms with Chinese interiors in a 43-story high-rise atop a Taipei metro station. 201 Tun Hwa South Rd.; 866/565-5050 or 886/2/2378-8888; shangri-la.com; doubles from $$

THAILAND

BANGKOK

Arun Residence Eclectic Asian- and European-inflected décor in a quaint 4-story property that has panoramic views of Wat Arun. Maharat Rd., 36-38 Soi Pratoo Nok Yoong; 66-2/221-9158; arunresidence.com; doubles from $

BANGKOK

The Conrad A tower oriented toward business travelers in the city's central financial district. 87 Wireless Rd.; 800/560-7966 or 66-2/690-9999; conradhotels.com; doubles from $

BANGKOK

The Eugenia A genteel colonial mansion with antiques and animal trophies. 267 Sukhumvit Rd., Soi 31; 66-2/259-9011; theeugenia.com; doubles from $

BANGKOK

Four Seasons Hotel Hand-painted silk ceilings and koi-filled waterways set apart a stately low-rise between the city's financial center and Lumpini Park. 155 Rajadamri Rd.; 800/332-3442 or 66-2/250-1000; fourseasons.com; doubles from $$

BANGKOK

Grand Hyatt Erawan A tranquil oasis near shopping and the Erawan Shrine. 494 Rajdamri Rd.; 800/233-1234 or 66-2/254-1234; grandhyatt.com; doubles from $

BANGKOK

JW Marriott Well-appointed and colorful rooms on Sukhumvit Road, Bangkok's lively restaurant and nightlife district. 4 Sukhumvit Rd., Soi 2; 800/228-9290 or 66-2/656-7700; marriott.com; doubles from $

BANGKOK

Luxx Polished studio-style rooms in an intimate hotel

off Silom Road. 6/11 Decho Rd., Bangruk; 66-2/635-8800; staywith luxx.com; doubles from $

BANGKOK

The Oriental 1887 legend with a modern addition, on the banks of the Chao Phraya River. 48 Oriental Ave.; 800/526-6566 or 66-2/659-9000; mandarin oriental.com; doubles from $$

BANGKOK

Peninsula Bangkok Asian-accented interiors in a sharp 37-story tower with river views. 333 Charoennakorn Rd.; 866/382-8388 or 66-2/861-2888; peninsula.com; doubles from $$

BANGKOK

Royal Orchid Sheraton Hotel & Towers River-front hotel, a short boat ride from the Grand Palace. 2 Charoen Krung Rd., Soi 30; 800/325-3535 or 66-2/266-0123; sheraton.com; doubles from $

BANGKOK

Shangri-La Hotel Expansive complex with tropical gardens, adjacent to the Skytrain. New Rd., 89 Soi Wat Suan Plu; 866/

565-5050 or 66-2/236-7777; shangri-la.com; doubles from $$

CHIANG MAI

Four Seasons Resort Cluster of Thai pavilions—each with a covered veranda—surrounded by rice paddies in the idyllic Mae Rim Valley. 800/332-3442 or 66-53/298-181; four seasons.com; doubles from $$$

CHIANG MAI

Mandarin Oriental Dhara Dhevi Sixty-acre contemporary resort built to resemble a Lanna village, just outside the city. 800/526-6566 or 66-53/888-888; mandarin oriental.com; doubles from $$

HUA HIN

Chiva-Som International Health Resort Beachfront haven with an extensive health and wellness menu on the Gulf of Thailand. 66-32/536-536; chivasom.com; rates from $$, per person, all-inclusive

KOH SAMUI

Four Seasons Resort Elegant villas with infinity pools overlooking the Gulf of Thailand. 800/332-3442 or 66-77/243-000; four

seasons.com; doubles from $$$

PHUKET

Amanpuri An understated and secluded resort set in a coconut grove above Pansea Beach. 800/477-9180 or 66-76/324-333; amanresorts.com; doubles from $$$

PHUKET

Banyan Tree Luxe Thai-style villas with open-air bathtubs and private gardens among the lagoons of Bang Tao Bay. 800/223-6800 or 66-76/324-374; banyantree.com; doubles from $$$

PHUKET

Indigo Pearl Industrial-chic complex on the site of a former tin mine. 66-76/327-006; indigo-pearl.com; doubles from $

PHUKET

JW Marriott Resort & Spa Family-friendly resort with tropical gardens, on Mai Khao Beach. 800/228-9290 or 66-76/338-000; jwmarriott.com; doubles from $$$

VIETNAM

HANOI

Sofitel Metropole Historic French-colonial hotel

between Hoan Kiem Lake and the Opera House. 15 Ngo Quyen St.; 800/763-4835 or 84-4/826-6919; sofitel.com; doubles from $$

HO CHI MINH CITY

Park Hyatt Saigon French colonial-inspired building with refined touches, overlooking the Opera House. 800/233-1234 or 84-8/824-1234; parkhyatt.com; doubles from $$

HOI AN

Nam Hai A collection of luxuriously spare free-standing villas on the South China Sea. 84-510/940-000; ghmhotels.com; doubles from $$$$

NHA TRANG

Evason Ana Mandara Resort & Six Senses Spa Beachside Vietnamese-style village off the famed Tran Phu Boulevard. 800/337-4685 or 84-58/524-705; six-senses.com; doubles from $$

PHU QUOC

La Veranda Grand Mercure Resort & Spa French colonial–style retreat on an under-the-radar island. 800/221-4542 or 84-77/982-988; laverandaresort.com; doubles from $$

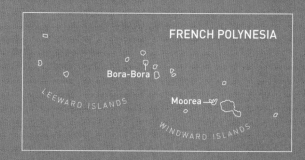

FRENCH POLYNESIA

Bora-Bora

Moorea

LEEWARD ISLANDS

WINDWARD ISLANDS

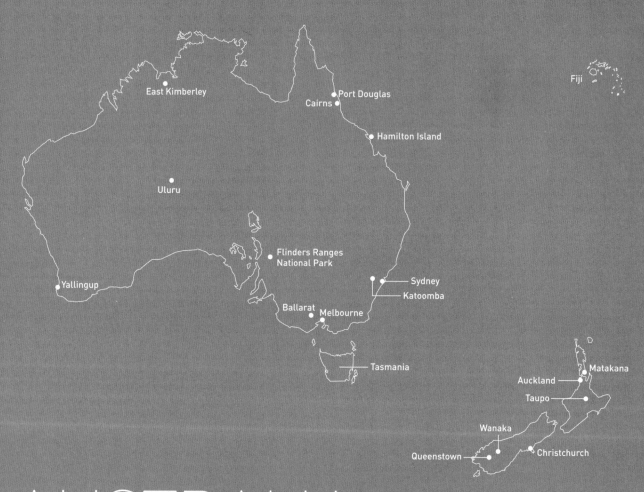

East Kimberley

Port Douglas
Cairns

Hamilton Island

Uluru

Fiji

Flinders Ranges
National Park

Yallingup

Sydney
Katoomba

Ballarat
Melbourne

Tasmania

Matakana
Auckland
Taupo

Wanaka
Christchurch
Queenstown

AUSTRALIA+
NEW ZEALAND+
THE SOUTH PACIFIC

AUSTRALIA

BALLARAT

Craig's Royal Hotel
Recently renovated
Victorian-era landmark in
downtown's historic district.
10 Lydiard St. S.; 61-3/5331-
1377; craigsroyal.com.au;
doubles from $

CAIRNS

Kewarra Beach Resort
A lodge and beachfront
bungalows set amid tropical
grounds near the Great
Barrier Reef. 61-7/4057-
6666; kewarra.com; doubles
from $$

EAST KIMBERLEY

El Questro Homestead
Outback retreat with Asian-
inspired rooms cantelvered
above the Chamberlain
Gorge. 61-8/9169-1777;
elquestrohomestead.com.
au; doubles from $$$$$

FLINDERS RANGES
NATIONAL PARK

Rawnsley Park Station
Luxury four-villa eco-lodge
near a 367-square-mile
nature preserve. 61-8/
8648-0030; rawnsleypark.
com.au; doubles from $$,
including breakfast

GREAT BARRIER REEF

Qualia New resort with
richly furnished pavilions
overlooking the Coral
Sea on Hamilton Island.
61-2/9433-3349;
qualiaresort.com; doubles
from $$$$$

KATOOMBA

**Lilianfels Blue Mountains
Resort & Spa** 1889 country
house with English gardens
and décor, on a bluff above
the Jamison Valley. 800/
237-1236 or 61-2/4780-
1200; lilianfels.com.au;
doubles from $$$

MELBOURNE

Grand Hyatt Curving
33-story tower with Art
Deco–inspired interiors.
123 Collins St.; 800/233-
1234 or 61-3/9657-1234;
hyatt.com; doubles from $

MELBOURNE

Langham Hotel Modern
riverside offshoot of the
London landmark. 1
Southgate Ave., Southbank;
61-3/8696-8888; langham
hotelmelbourne.com.au;
doubles from $$

MELBOURNE

Park Hyatt Discreet hotel
with marble lobby,
next to the Fitzroy Gardens.
1 Parliament Square;
800/233-1234 or 61-3/
9224-1234; hyatt.com;
doubles from $$

MELBOURNE

Sofitel Minimalist guest
rooms in a downtown

hotel within walking
distance of great shopping.
25 Collins St.; 800/763-4835
or 61-3/9653-0000; sofitel
melbourne.com.au; doubles
from $$

PORT DOUGLAS

**Mantra Treetops Resort &
Spa** Rain forest–shaded
refuge with contemporary
guest rooms near Four Mile
Beach. 61-7/4030-4333;
mantratreetops.com.au;
doubles from $

SYDNEY

Four Seasons Hotel
Downtown hotel between
business and leisure
districts. 199 George St.;
800/332-3442 or 61-2/
9238-0000; fourseasons.
com; doubles from $$

SYDNEY

The InterContinental
Smartly refurbished tower
rising above the 19th-
century façade of the
former Treasury Building.
Bridge and Phillip Sts.;
800/327-0200 or 61-2/9253-
9000; ichotelsgroup.com;
doubles from $$

SYDNEY

Observatory Hotel
Discreet property with
grand 19th-century style,
in the Rocks district.
89-113 Kent St.; 800/237-
1236 or 61-2/9256-2222;

observatoryhotel.com.au;
doubles from $$

SYDNEY

Park Hyatt Art-filled
waterfront outpost with
opera house and Harbour
Bridge views. 7 Hickson
Rd.; 800/233-1234 or
61-2/9241-1234; hyatt.com;
doubles from $$$

SYDNEY

Shangri-La Hotel Smartly
designed hotel in the
Central Business District.
176 Cumberland St.;
866/565-5050 or 61-2/
9250-6000; shangri-la.com;
doubles from $$

SYDNEY

The Westin Tailored guest
rooms in a skyscraper
that's been added on to the
former post office. 1 Martin
Place; 800/228-3000 or
61-2/8223-1111; westin.
com.au; doubles from $$

TASMANIA

**Voyages Cradle Mountain
Lodge** Timber cabins in the
Tasmanian wilderness at
the edge of Lake St. Clair
National Park. 61-2/8296-
8010 or 613/6492-1303;
voyages.com.au; doubles
from $

ULURU

Voyages Longitude 131°
Palatial tents on an

isolated sand dune in the outback. 800/525-4800 or 61-2/8296-8010; voyages.com.au; doubles from $$$$$

YALLINGUP
Moondance Lodge A streamlined wine-country haven built from local materials, close to the Margaret River. 61-8/9750-1777; moondancelodge.com; doubles from $$, including breakfast

FIJI
DENARAU ISLAND
Sheraton Fiji Resort Beachside complex with a laid-back vibe. The hotel will be closed from May 1 to November 1 for renovations. 800/325-3535 or 011-679/675-0777; sheraton.com; doubles from $

DENARAU ISLAND
Westin Resort & Spa Collection of Asian-inspired open-air pavilions on a private beach. 800/228-3000 or 679/675-0000; westin.com; doubles from $$

FRENCH POLYNESIA
BORA-BORA
Bora Bora Lagoon Resort & Spa Elegant thatched bungalows surrounded by crystal-clear lagoons. 800/237-1236 or 689/604-000; boraboralagoon.com; doubles from $$$

BORA-BORA
Hotel Bora Bora Historic French Polynesian resort that blends a relaxed South Pacific décor and polished Aman style. 800/477-9180 or 011-689/604-460; amanresorts.com; doubles from $$$

MOOREA
InterContinental Resort & Spa Austerely furnished bungalows along a hillside and lagoon on the north-west coast of the island. 800/327-0200 or 689/604-900; intercontinental.com; doubles from $$

MOOREA
Moorea Pearl Resort & Spa Traditional Polynesian-style bungalows on stilts above the water and lining a white-sand beach. 800/657-3275 or 689/551-750; pearlresorts.com; doubles from $$

NEW ZEALAND
AUCKLAND
Hilton Gleaming white complex on Princes Wharf near the business district and Sky City Tower. 147 Quay St.; 800/445-8667 or 649/978-2000; hilton.com; doubles from $$

CHRISTCHURCH
The George Design-centric outpost on Hagley Park and the Avon River. 800/525-4800 or 64-3/379 4560; thegeorge.com; doubles from $$

MATAKANA
Takatu Lodge & Vineyard Modern guesthouse, part of a wine-making estate in a picturesque North Island valley. 64-9/423-0299; takatulodge.co.nz; doubles from $$, including breakfast

QUEENSTOWN
Millbrook French provincial–style escape in an alpine amphitheater. 64-3/441-7000; millbrook.co.nz; doubles from $$, including breakfast

TAUPO
Huka Lodge Renowned fishing retreat on the banks of the North Island's Waikato River. 800/525-4800 or 64-7/378-5791; hukalodge.com; doubles from $$$$$, including meals

WANAKA
Whare Kea Lodge Luminous steel-and-glass oasis on the South Island overlooking Lake Wanaka. 800/735-2478 or 64-3/443-1400; wharekealodge.com; doubles from $$$$$, including some meals

Whare Kea Lodge,
on Lake Wanaka, in
New Zealand.

TRIPS DIRECTORY

A room at
Villa Pisani, in Italy's
Veneto region.

A bedroom
at Verana,
in Yelapa,
Mexico.

HOTELS INDEX

A member of the
staff on the grounds of
the Chedi Muscat.

A sitting
area at the
Hotel
Antumalal,
in Chile.

GEOGRAPHIC INDEX

CONTRIBUTORS

Richard Alleman
Adam Baer
Luke Barr
Raul Barreneche
Caroline Baum
Alan Brown
Paul Chai
Aric Chen
Aaron Clark
Marcelle Clements
Douglas Cooper
Anthony Dennis
Bill Donahue
Claire Downey
Charlotte Druckman
Florence Fabricant

Amy Farley
Andrew Ferren
Eleni N. Gage
Charles Gandee
Jaime Gross
Darrell Hartman
Mark Healy
Latilla Isaac
Karrie Jacobs
Sarah Kantrowitz
David Kaufman
Melik Kaylan
David A. Keeps
Stirling Kelso

Matt Lee
Ted Lee
Shana Liebman
Peter Jon Lindberg
Alexandra Marshall
Ralph Martin
Mario R. Mercado
Robert Milliken
Shane Mitchell
John Newton
Danielle Pergament
Christopher Petkanas
Amy E. Robertson
Douglas Rogers
Rory Ross
Julian Rubinstein

Guy Saddy
Bruce Schoenfeld
John Seabrook
Dan Shaw
Maria Shollenbarger
Valerie Stivers-Isakova
Guy Trebay
Alison Tyler
Leisa Tyler
Valerie Waterhouse
Sally Webb
Nina Willdorf
Jeff Wise

PHOTOGRAPHERS